PARAROCHIAL BENEFICES IN THE NEW CODE

A DISSERTATION

Submitted to the Faculty of Sacred Sciences of the Catholic University of America in partial fulfilment of the requirements for the Degree of Doctorate in Canon Law

By

HENRY FRANCIS GOLDEN

Priest of the Archdiocese of Philadelphia

[1921]

TABLE OF CONTENTS

TABLE OF CONTENTS

INTRODUCTION.

The subject of benefices has not hitherto been of much practical importance for us in this country on account of the missionary status of our parishes. A distinguished canonist of this country sums up the situation preceding the Code as follows:

"In the United States benefices are almost unknown. A solitary example in New Orleans figured as a notable exception in the decree of the Second Plenary Council. A few parochial benefices are found in the Province of San Francisco, and there is good ground for the opinion which sees in permanent rectorships all the requisites of a benefice; but these instances, with the episcopates, are in marked contrast with the general organization of the Church in the United States."[1]

Until 1908 we lived as a missionary country in all respects, under the jurisdiction of the Propaganda. In 1908, we were removed from the competence of this congregation and placed under the common law, but we still retained our missionary parishes. It is true that wherever the common law obtains, the erection of canonical parishes and benefices is the rule, but it required the promulgation of the Code to verify this condition here. The reasons for this exception will be discussed when we treat of the present state of our parishes, in the last chapter of this dissertation.

Now that it is certain, both from the words of the Code and their official interpretation as applied to us, that our parishes have attained the canonical status desired by law, and are benefices, it is of practical aid

---

1. Creag, *Catholic Encyclopedia, Article "Benefice,"* New York, 1911.

to priests to know something concerning benefices. In this work we do not intend to discuss the whole field of benefices, but only a very limited part of that field, namely, that of parochial benefices. These are the usual benefices found in any country, but in this country they are the only kind seen, with the exception of the episcopates. Not an inconsiderable part, however, of the Code legislation on benefices, concerns the right of patronage, which is entirely lacking in the United States, and concerning which no mention will be made hereafter in this discussion. Those other forms of benefices, namely, those to which are not attached the care of souls, will be considered in passing, our main purpose being the question of parochial benefices.

As the subject of benefices is dealt with by the Code in conjunction with that of parishes, it will be necessary, for the right understanding of benefices, to draw upon the legislation concerning parishes, and some of this legislation is not entirely new. Our missionary parishes, while not canonical, were, nevertheless, governed by a law which approached, as far as possible, the common law. Where the new law makes a change in the old discipline, we shall note the difference.

CHAPTER I

Nature and Species of Benefices

1. *Origin of Name*

The term "Benefice" had its origin, it seems, in those grants of land made in the sixth century or shortly after, by the civil princes to their soldiers, either in reward for their services, or on condition that these soldiers serve them in war or in peace. These public estates, which, in the language of the Franks and Lombards, were called fiefs, in the Latin language were called *beneficia*, as held of the prince's bounty. From the resemblance between these civil estates and ecclesiastical estates given clerics for their support, the latter were also called benefices. The analogy is very strong, as the clergy could be considered as soldiers who wage a spiritual warfare under the direction of their bishops.

2. *Definition of a Benefice*

What, then, is a benefice? It is defined: "A juridical entity, established or erected in perpetuity by competent ecclesiastical authority, consisting of a sacred office and the right to receive the revenue connected with the office or foundation."[2] This definition of the Code is different from any of the definitions given by the authors prior to the Code, and settles some questions upon which the authors could not agree. It has also enlarged the idea of benefices, making it applicable to many entities which were not included under the old idea of a benefice; thus making it more easy to erect

2. Canon 1409.

parishes into benefices. The definition received as the standard prior to the Code was "The perpetual right to receive the fruit from the goods of a church, on account of the holding of a spiritual office, which right was constituted or established by ecclesiastical authority."[3]

The first change we notice, then, is in the perpetuity of a benefice. Perpetuity is two-fold: objective and subjective. The first kind of perpetuity is that the benefice is perpetual insofar that the benefice, once established, always remains, even after the beneficiary dies, so that after his death it can be given to another. In the second sense a benefice is perpetual insofar that he who possesses it may not be deprived of it unless he freely give it up, or is removed from it by judicial trial or by that administrative form of removal recognized in certain cases by law.

Before the Code the authors were divided as to whether both objective and subjective perpetuity were necessary, or whether objective perpetuity sufficed in benefices. Sebastianelli held that the two-fold perpetuity must be demanded according to the laws of the Church, although he confesses that certain institutions are called benefices which lack the subjective element, and others which lacked the objective element. According to this author these were called benefices, but not properly so on account of the lack of the two-fold element of perpetuity. This view was held also by other recognized authors.[4]

On the other hand, there were not lacking authors of repute who held that although the two-fold species of perpetuity was the usual thing, nevertheless the idea of subjective perpetuity was not so essential that it always forbade the conferring of a benefice in a revokable way. This was really deviating from the very definition given

3. Ojetti, "*Synopsis Rerum Moralium et Juris Pontificii,*" Romae, 1909.
4. Bargilliat, "*Praelectiones Juris Canonici,*" Vol. II, No. 1383, Parisiis, 1915.

by the canonists, namely, the perpetual right to receive the fruit.

Wernz[5] says that if the perpetual right to the revenue be lacking, "*sane beneficum ecclesiasticum non est*," but that manual benefices are to be considered true benefices in favorable things unless a special exception be proved.

The Code in canon 1409, above quoted, has settled the question by omitting the necessity of subjective perpetuity, and making the essence of the benefice to consist in the juridical entity with objective perpetuity, and considering manual or subjectively temporary benefices as true benefices.

Another of the questions settled by the Code deals with the formal object of benefices. Some said that the formal object was the right to receive the fruits.[6] Others found the formal object in the spiritual office to which they attached the right to the revenue.[7] This last doctrine was used more by theologians than by canonists, and deviated from the original idea of a benefice, as well as from the doctrine of the canons which constituted the benefice from two elements, namely, the sacred office and the right to the revenue, from the union of which two elements we get a benefice. Boniface VIII gives the axiom: "*Beneficium datur propter officium sacrum*."[8] Innocent III tells us that benefices were established and given to certain persons so that they could continually serve in the churches. And the Fathers of Trent[9] have given the principle: "*beneficia ad divinum cultum, atque ecclesiastica munia obeunda esse constituta.*" The spiritual office, therefore, is not the

5. *Jus Decretalium*, Vol. II, No. 240, Prati, 1915.
6. Sebastianelli, "*Praelectiones Juris Canonici*" *Vol "De Rebus*," No. 184, Romae, 1905.
7. Cr. Vecchiotti, "*Institutiones Canonicae*, Vol. II, page 25, Augustae Taurinorum, 1886.
8. Cap. 15, Tit. III, Lib. I in VI.
9. Sess. XXI, c. 3, de ref.

principal part of the benefice to which is added the right to receive the revenue as something secondary.

The first opinion which found the formal object in the right to the revenue was, then, the correct one, because the Church, in order to insure the more permanent performance of sacred functions in the different churches established the foundation, or dos, which yielded sufficient revenue annually to support decently a cleric. This *foundation* usually consisted of immovable property or real estate, but could also be movable goods, provided they were certain and stable. The revenue, then, usually consisted of the fruits of the lands, or the interest on the bonds or mortgages, or even a certain sum of money paid, for instance, by the Government, as is the case in Belgium.[10]

A benefice, therefore, is a juridical entity established or erected in perpetuity by competent ecclesiastical authority, consisting of a sacred office, and the right to certain revenue. Three things in this new idea of a benefice stand out prominently; viz.: the intervention of ecclesiastical authority, the sacred office and the revenue from the foundation attached to the office. These are not new requirements, although the definition has been revised with regard to the perpetuity required; and the revenue to be made into a foundation has been extended so as to include several classes not hitherto possible as beneficial revenue.

3. *Intervention of Ecclesiastical Authority in Erecting Benefices*

The necessity of the intervention of ecclesiastical authority in the erection of ecclesiastical benefices comes from the very nature of benefices. For the benefice denotes the right to the revenue from *ecclesiastical*

10. Smith, "*Compendium Juris Canonici,*" No. 986, 4th Edition, New York, 1890.

goods, or from goods which are in the patrimony of the Church. But nothing can be conceived to be in the patrimony of the Church without the consent of the Church. Moreover, one who wishes to found a benefice asks of the Church that certain sacred functions desired by him be performed by the Church, and that She do this by appointing a cleric to do it. The Church cannot be obliged to do these things without Her own consent.

It makes little difference whether the Church gives consent to the erection expressly, tacitly or only presumedly. Express consent is had when the Church expressly says that She approves the pious act of the founder. She is considered as consenting tacitly when, for example, a bishop would appoint a cleric to a benefice not yet canonically erected, or would in some similar way demonstrate his wish. Presumed consent was frequent in ancient benefices, and in sending a cleric to the benefice, it was presumed that ecclesiastical authority had intervened.

Under the name of ecclesiastical authority, which should intervene in the erection of benefices, comes, in the first place, the Roman Pontiff. He has authority to erect benefices of all classes anywhere in the world, and certain forms of them cannot be erected by any inferior power, as in the case of a new diocese, or of a cathedral chapter.

For benefices inferior to the episcopacy, and not reserved to the Pope, the authority of the bishop is sufficient to erect benefices. This is clear not only from canon 1414, 2; but also from long standing and constant discipline in the Church, nor is it clear that this power was ever denied bishops by the Church. According to the above mentioned canon, cardinals can erect simple benefices in the Church given them in Rome as their titular Church, provided that this Church does not belong to exempt religious.

4. *The Sacred Office*

The second requisite in the erection of benefices is the sacred office, and this can be defined, according to canon 145, as a position permanently established, either by divine or ecclesiastical law, which is conferred according to the regulations of canon law, and which enjoys some participation in ecclesiastical power, either of Orders or of jurisdiction. From this definition we see that a benefice, by being an ecclesiastical office, must be conferred according to the rules of canon law, and not arbitrarily. An example of an office established by divine law is that of the episcopate; one of ecclesiastical law is that of the pastorate because the Apostles were made bishops by Christ Himself, while parishes did not originate until after several centuries. An instance of an office enjoying some participation in ecclesiastical power of Orders is that of a benefice to which is attached the sole duty of celebrating Mass; while a parochial benefice includes at least some ecclesiastical jurisdiction.

A benefice, therefore, is an ecclesiastical office and must be governed not only by the canons in the third book of the Code, but also by those in the second book applying to ecclesiastical offices.

5. *The Right to Revenue*

The third requisite in the erection of a benefice is the right to the revenue attached to it. The word right bears special emphasis in this connection because a beneficiary has the right, even though, for example, a government has taken away its property and the cleric therefore receives no revenue. The institution remains a benefice as long as the cleric in charge has the right.

As said above, the revenue of a benefice may come from a foundation or may be a certain amount of money paid periodically by some moral person, or even may be the offerings of the faithful. Canon 1410 gives the definition of what may constitute the endowment, and this question of endowment has undergone even greater change than the definition of the benefice. The canon says: "The endowment of a benefice is constituted either by property, the ownership of which belongs to the juridical entity itself, or by certain and voluntary offerings of the faithful, which belong to the rector of the benefice, or, as they are called, stole fees within the limits of diocesan taxation or legitimate custom, or by choral distributions, exclusive of a third part of the same, if all the revenues of the benefice consist of choral distribution." The change in this definition of endowment consists in the extension of it to sources of revenue formerly considered outside the range of endowment of a benefice. Of course, the endowment consisting of property, the fruit of which goes to the beneficiary, is the oldest and the classic definition. The very name benefice as applied to ecclesiastical institutions, took its original from the fact that they resembled the grants of land conceded by civil princes to their subjects.

Neither is there anything new in the endowment consisting in the payment by any family or moral person, for the Holy See has many times declared that these have the requisites for beneficial revenue. We see an example of this form of endowment in Belgium, where the government pays a certain sum at stated times to the pastors. In France, where the government has confiscated ecclesiastical property, this is practiced also by the government.

The third form of endowment, namely, certain and voluntary offerings of the faithful, that belong to the rector, is an addition to the old idea of revenue. Some authors, before the Code, admitted that offerings of the faithful imposed as a tax could be constituted as revenue of a benefice, but none held that the *voluntary* offerings could be so constituted. Bargilliat[11] and Wernz[12] held

---

11. *Op. cit.*, No. 1384 B.
12. *Op. cit.*, Vol. III, No. 180, 1901.

this with regard to offerings imposed as a tax on the faithful. But now the *free* offerings can be constituted by the bishop as a true source of revenue in the erection of a benefice, and it is to be noted that this fact will make it very much easier to prove the existence of benefices in this country where the usual revenue of parishes comes from the free offerings and stole fees.

The question of stole fees was a disputed one before the Code, and we find authors on both sides. Bargilliat[13] says that as stole fees are not a stipend for a determined work, nor a mere honorarium, but are part of the support due the pastor, and which must be given according to law, they can be counted among the revenue of the beneficiary. Others thought that on account of the uncertainty of them they could not be classed as beneficial revenue. De Lugo held that even these, when uncertain, in the sense that the amount could not be determined beforehand, could be considered under this head. The Rota decided that stole fees might be so held but that the bishops should establish the amount sufficient. Now the clear definition of the Code leaves no doubt about the matter.

The last change in the definition of endowment regards choral distribution. These distributions are strangers to our American institutions and so a word about them may not be out of place. Choral distributions signify a certain revenue distributed daily to the members of the cathedral or collegiate chapter who are actually present at the divine service or who are considered present by a fiction of the law. Canon 420 gives the list of those considered present *ex fictions juris.* This distribution had its original with Yvo of Chartres, who, in order to insure the presence of the members of the chapter at divine services, daily distributed the revenue of a certain benefice among those present as a sort of extra inducement for their presence. Whoever was

13. *Op. cit., ibidem.*

absent, therefore, lost a certain amount of revenue, and it was divided among the members present. Later the Council of Trent[14] ordered bishops to set aside the third part of all the fruits, revenues and income from all the prebends for daily distribution among those personally and actively assisting at the divine offices. Trent also declared[15] that where there were no choral distributions, or only such as were negligible, the bishop should set aside the third part of all the profits, incomes and revenues received from the dignities, canonships, offices and other church benefices, and turn them into daily distribution. Canon 395 repeats this law of Trent.

But now these choral distributions may become the revenue of a benefice instead of merely an additional to the revenue of the chapter. This may happen, for example, only when there is nothing left of the benefices held by the members of the chapter but the choral distribution, that is, when the chapter holds no benefices in the old sense of the word. In this case, the original idea of distribution, namely, the reward for assistance at services is provided for by the law that the one-third of the choral distribution, now made into the endowment, shall be reserved for daily choral distribution to the members present, while the other two-thirds belongs to them regardless of presence. So this choral distribution, after becoming the endowment of the members, loses the old idea of choral distribution while the third withdrawn from it fills the place of it. As we have no cathedral or collegiate chapters in the United States, the question of choral distributions has not any practical value at present for us.

6. *Species of Benefices.*

After having seen something of the origin of benefices and the essential characteristics of a true

---

14. Sess. XXI, c. 3, de ref.
15. Ibid.

benefice, we will next consider the different kinds of benefices. In this matter the Code has, in the main, followed the doctrine of the authors but by authoritatively naming all the possible species, it has eliminated the arbitrary classification hitherto found among the canonists, so that in the future we shall have a certain definite number and no more, and each class will be defined exactly, without the confusion found in pre-Code authors.

The first class named by the Code are *Consistorial* and *Non-Consistorial,* according as they are conferred in Consistory or otherwise. Consistorial benefices are those which were called by the authors major benefices, that is, having perfect and complete jurisdiction—legislative, judicial and coactive power. Bishoprics are the usual examples of this form. All other benefices are non-Consistorial.

The second distinction is into *secular* and *religious* benefices, according as they belong to seculars, or to religious. When there is any doubt whether a benefice is secular or religious, it must be presumed to be secular when it is erected outside religious houses or churches. This ruling of the Code has settled a point upon which almost all the authors erred; for they said that in doubt, all benefices are presumed to be secular until the contrary is proved, omitting the distinction between benefices founded within and without religious houses. Sebastianelli was the only one to point out this difference.

The third division of benefices is into *double* or *residential,* and *simple* or *non-residential* benefices, according as they have the obligation of residence along with the sacred office, or not. In the beginning there were no non-residential benefices, but every cleric who was ordained was assigned to some particular church. Ordination and assignment to some church were considered almost inseparable. But in the course of time the bishops began to ordain men without a title of support because they had no benefice vacant and were afraid of losing the men. Of course this was contrary to the canons. The only way, then, of supporting these men was to assign them some office other than the care of souls, or to make them coadjutors to some beneficiary. Thus simple benefices came into existence, and when these were not sufficient to support the cleric, the bishop assigned him a pension, or else the cleric lived on his patrimony.[16] The parochial benefice is the ordinary example of a residential benefice; while a Mass foundation, erected by a bishop, and given for life to a cleric, is an example of a simple benefice.

The next form of benefices given by canon 1411 is the *manual, temporal* or *revokable* benefice, as contrasted with the *perpetual* or *irremovable* benefice. The distinction between these benefices is the subjective perpetuity about which we spoke above. The authors called the perpetual benefices the *titulata*, or given in title, and the others manual, but declared that the latter kind were not strictly benefices. In the Code all secular benefices are perpetual, while all religious benefices are manual. Canon 1438 tells us that all secular benefices must be conferred for life unless the law of foundation, immemorial custom or particular indult makes it otherwise. And Canon 454 rules that all pastors should be permanent, although religious pastors are revokable at the will of either the bishop or their superior. This irremovability of secular pastors does not mean that they cannot be moved, but that they cannot be moved except for reasons and by the procedure expressed in the law. The words removable and irremovable can be a source of confusion because, in treating of benefices, all secular benefices are conferred for life, that is, they

16. Wernz, *op. cit.*, Vol. II, No. 245.

are irremovable, while in the second book of the Code the law says that all secular pastors are either irremovable or removable, thus apparently contradicting the law on benefices. The terms removable and irremovable have a more specific meaning when applied to pastors than when applied to benefices in general. They denote a difference in degree of stability and a more intricate process of law required to remove the one than the other. Both species of parish are given for life and the pastor cannot be removed at will, but only according to the direction of the law. A removable pastor is only so-called because a less involved process is required to remove him than the so-called irremovable pastor. It is more confusing because this division of pastors into removable and irremovable species is newly introduced by the Code. Prior to the Code all canonical pastors were irremovable and the process for removal was the same for all, excepting, of course, the removable at will pastors which obtained in France after the Revolution, and in some parts of Latin America by Apostolic Indult. It would seem that even these removable at will pastors were abolished in 1910 by the *Maxima Cura*, so that immediately before the Code all pastors were irremovable. It might have been clearer if the Code had used the words removable and irremovable with regard to pastors, and perpetual and temporary with regard to benefices. For in benefices, the only kind of beneficiaries who are removable are the religious, while with regard to parishes, even seculars may be removable.

The final division of benefices is into those *having the care of souls* and those *not having the care of souls.* The parochial benefice is an example of the first kind, while the office of canon in a cathedral chapter would be an example of the second species. In the United States there are no *non-curata* benefices, the only benefices being those of bishops and pastors.

7. *Offices Resembling Benefices*

The above named five species are the only possible kinds of benefices, although certain other offices have some similarity to them. Canon 1412 gives us a list of these offices, and the first among them is the parochial vicariate not permanently erected. It is evident that objective perpetuity is lacking in these vicariates and hence the idea of a true benefice is destroyed.

Lay chaplaincies also give some semblance to benefices. A lay chaplaincy may be defined as the obligation either of celebrating Mass or of performing certain duties in a certain chapel on certain days and hours, established without the intervention of ecclesiastical authority. The lacking essential is the intervention of ecclesiastical authority, and if it had this requisite, together with objective perpetuity, it would be a true benefice.

Coadjutors also have some likeness to benefices but are lacking in so much that they have not the title, or, in other words, do not possess the benefice in their own name. This applies to both coadjutors with succession, and coadjutors without succession.

Personal pensions, although they give a cleric a right to certain revenue, are not benefices. They may be defined as a certain part of the fruit separated from any benefice, episcopal table or abbacy by legitimate authority for a time, and not perpetually.[17] These are usually given to pastors removed from their parish and are not benefices because they lack both the sacred office and the objective perpetuity.

Finally, temporary Commenda, or grants of income from the property of a church or monastery made to a cleric on condition that if he lose his claim, the revenues shall revert to the church or monastery, are not to be

---

17. Santi, *op. cit.*, Tit. V, No. 35. Santi-Leitner, "*Praelectiones Juris Canonicae*," Ratisbonae, 1898.

considered benefices. These have neither the sacred office nor the objective perpetuity required to make them benefices. The term Commenda is generally used to designate the custody of a church or benefice. In ancient times it was the custody of a vacant church, not perpetually, but only for a time; indeed it was not conceded for more than six months. Later the custom arose of conferring this custody perpetually *ad instar tituli* and so the cleric possessing the title had a true benefice. Trent,[18] in order to stop the abuse of one cleric having a plurality of benefices, legislated that nobody in the future could hold more than one benefice, even if one was in title and the other *in commendam,* except in the case where the one was insufficient for his decent support, in which supposition, the cleric could be given another benefice, as long as both benefices did not require personal residence. This law of Trent is repeated in canon 1439, which says that nobody can possess a plurality of benefices, either in title or *in commendam,* and defines plurality as both the holding of two benefices, one of which is sufficient for decent support. Therefore, if a cleric has one benefice which is not sufficient for his support, and he can likewise perform the duties of another benefice, for example, a simple benefice, the Ordinary is not forbidden to grant him the second benefice. By the law of Trent a cleric cannot possess more than two benefices, even if he cannot be supported from both of them, and as the Code legislation is merely a repetition of the law of Trent, so we must interpret it in the same way, and say that two is the highest number of benefices which may be possessed by any one cleric without the express permission of the Holy See.

---

18. Sess. VII, 2, 4 and Sess. XXIV, 17.

CHAPTER II

Erection of Benefices

1. *Power of Bishops to Erect*

We have seen that the ecclesiastical authority must intervene in the erection of a benefice. We have also seen that the Sovereign Pontiff, by virtue of his plenitude of power, can erect benefices of any nature, in any part of the world, and to him alone is reserved the erection of certain forms of benefices. And as he is above all canon law, he is not bound by its prescriptions except insofar as they are declarations of the divine law.

For other benefices beneath the episcopacy and that of the cathedral chapter, the authority of the Ordinary is sufficient whether the Ordinary be a bishop or an inferior prelate having quasi-episcopal authority. This is drawn from the constant and long standing discipline of the Church. For in former times, by the authority of the bishop, clergy were deputed to perform certain sacred functions and on account of them they received the revenue necessary for their support. During the course of time, after the clergy ceased to live a common life, the bishops themselves distributed the immovable goods of the churches to each of the clergy serving the churches, so that each one received in perpetuity a certain portion of the ecclesiastical goods by reason of this office, to possess and administer. Many canons gave this power to bishops. Trent openly did this when it commanded Ordinaries to create in their major churches canon theologians and penitentiaries, which precept certainly supposes that the Fathers of Trent recognized this power in bishops. The law, therefore, with regard to erection, has not been changed, and whatever could be done by Ordinaries under the old law, still applies in the new.

2. *What Constitutes a Suitable Foundation*

Besides the ecclesiastical authority in erecting benefices, it is also required that a suitable foundation or means of support be at hand before the benefice may be erected.[19] The word suitable, or *congrua,* as the Latin has it, is a canonical term to designate the lowest sum proper for the yearly income of a cleric. On account of the many changes to which a benefice is liable, it became necessary for the ecclesiastical authorities to decree that first and foremost the proper sustenance for the beneficiary should be provided for and that a minimum revenue should be determined, below which his income was not to fall. This was all the more necessary in cases where the benefices were incorporated with monasteries or collegiate churches. Thus we see in the old canons a minimum amount was set down, which afterward became useless because of the changing values of currency. Trent[20] leaves the determination of the *congrua* to the judgment of the bishop. Wherefore, the bishop should examine whether the amount be suitable, taking into account the quality of the benefice, place, person and the other circumstances; from all of which facts he may determine whether or not the cleric can live decently on it. This amount must, of course, vary with the fluctuation of values at different times. It must not be so parsimoniously fixed as to provide for the beneficiary merely the necessaries of life. To be a proper income in accordance with the dignity of his state, it should likewise be sufficient to enable him to

19. 1415.
20. Sess. XXI, c. 4, De Ref.

dispense moderate hospitality and almsgiving, and supply himself with books and the like. The Council of Trent also said that about one-third should be given to the vicar.

When the suitable amount has been settled by the bishop, it is always presumed to be sufficient unless it is proved to have become insufficient, and in this case the burden of the proof is on the beneficiary. If, after erection, the amount does become insufficient, the bishop should unite another benefice to it, or provide otherwise, by a pension or by some other means; otherwise he should see to it that the benefice is suppressed.

If the endowment fund of the benefice is in money, the Ordinary—having heard the advice of the diocesan council of administration—will invest the money in safe and fruitful real estate or bonds and stocks of corporations that he can trust, or in the public debt bonds. The diocesan council of administration is a board consisting of the bishop and two or more members, to be appointed with the advice of the diocesan consulters, of which the bishop is the president. The institution of this board of advisers is obligatory unless its equivalent has already been provided for by law or peculiar custom.[21] The wisdom of seeking the advice of such a board of skilled men needs no comment. In questions of such endowment the whole future of the benefice depends on the wise investment of the funds and therefore no precaution is too great, especially when we consider the changing value of stocks, and even of real estate.

3. *Parishes Not Having Sufficient Endowment*

The third paragraph of canon 1415 says that the bishop is not forbidden to erect a parish, even if the endowment cannot be secured, provided that he prudently foresees that the necessaries will not be lacking

21. 1520.

from some other source. Such a case might happen when the parish is too small to provide sufficiently for the pastor; in this case the pastor may be given a *non-curata* benefice to supply the deficiency, or he may live on his patrimony, if he consents to so live, or the bishop may establish a missionary fund for the support of such poor localities. The question here arises whether or not these parishes or quasi-parishes are benefices. It is clear that if they are to be considered benefices, they are an exception to the general rule that a sufficient income must be provided by the benefice or some other moral person, according to canon 1410. On the other hand, the Code says that where the sufficient endowment is lacking, the Ordinary may erect *parishes or quasi-parishes*. It is true that the canonical legislation concerning benefices is part of the legislation relative to parishes, and that, as a rule, they are considered to be benefices. But is this identity necessary and inseparable? It was not so in the old law. Putzer[22] says, on the authority of Brabandere, that a parish could exist without being a benefice. Brabandere says that the entities are separable because the benefice is not necessary for the pastorate. His reason was that for a benefice, perpetuity was required, while for a parish perpetuity was not required, but only the obligation and right to exercise in one's own name the care of souls for a certain definite number of people who, in turn, are bound to receive the sacraments from him. Brabandere says this idea can be fulfilled even if the pastor be revokable *ad nutum*, and therefore not a benefice. This revokable pastor existed prior to the *Maxima Cura* in France.

Admitting that the revokable pastor no longer exists, nevertheless the argument for the separability of the two ideas may have some influence in determining whether

22. *Commentarium in Facultates Apostolicas*, p. 172, 1898.

or not the parishes and quasi-parishes mentioned in canon 1415, 3, are benefices. The Code, in canon 1423, speaks of parishes while discussing the union of *benefices,* so the mention of *parishes* in 1415 is not conclusive evidence that they are parishes and not benefices.

The only reason for thinking that the parishes of 1415 are not benefices is that they have not the required endowment, but even that is not conclusive, as the very mention of them under the subject of benefices may be sufficient to conclude that they are benefices by exception to the general rule. When canon 1412 speaks of certain institutions and offices which have certain similarity to benefices, without being true benefices, it does not mention this species of parish, and this may be used as an additional argument in favor of their status as benefices.

4. *Remaining Conditions for Erection*

Having established the fact of the endowment sufficient for the decent support of the clergy of the benefice, it is the duty of the bishop, before he erects the benefice, to invite and hear the opinions of all those who are interested, namely, parishioners and others who may have to contribute or who will probably suffer a detriment. However, the omission of this formality will not invalidate the establishment of the parish or benefice. The erection is then made by a legitimate document or public writing in which is defined the place, the revenue, rights and duties of the beneficiary, and this document is to be placed in the archives so as to be available in case of necessity to determine right in any conflicts which may arise. Just as the calling in of the interested parties is not necessary for validity, so also the drawing up in a public document of the fact of the erection is not for validity, and its omission will not affect the canonical status of the parish or benefice. It is well to note this fact because when we discuss the nature of the parishes in the United States, we shall see that they have not, so far, been erected formally into benefices, but having all the other qualities, they are true benefices for the reason that the decree of erection dos not affect their canonical status.

If the endowment fund is being supplied by some person, the Ordinary may permit him in the establishment to put into the agreement conditions which are contrary to common law, provided they are becoming, and not contrary to the idea of a benefice. This is not a new concession, as we see it as far back as the decretals, and it is given the founder on account of his generosity in establishing the benefice. However, the conditions must be possible, becoming, and must be admitted by the Ordinary. Conditions are acceptable which are not only not contrary to good morals, but also which would not exclude anything which would render the ministry less useful or less honorable. An example of a dishonest condition would be that irregular clergy be admitted to the benefice.

Once admitted by the bishop, the conditions cannot be changed validly by the Ordinary unless they be changes favorable to the Church and made with the consent of the founder or patron. The benefice is a bi-lateral contract between the Church and the founder, obliging each party in justice; and the consent of both must be had to change it. Since the Ordinary acts merely as the vicar or administrator of the Church in this matter, he has no other faculty than that conceded him by the Church, namely, changes favorable to the Church. It is also worthy of note that in the future no right of patronage may be given anyone, the only exception being that the founder have the right of nomianting the first beneficiary.[23]

---

23. 1450.

CHAPTER III

The Union of Benefices

After defining a benefice and legislating concerning its erection, the Code next treats the altering of a benefice which is already erected. This alteration is made in one of six ways, namely, by union, transfer, division, dismembration, conversion and by suppression. We will first consider the union of benefices as it is one of the most important means of altering a benefice, and the bulk of legislation concerning the alteration deals with union.

The union of a benefice may be defined as the connection of two or more benefices or churches made by legitimate superior authority,[24] and is either perpetual or temporary, according as it is made absolutely and without regard to persons, or is made for the lifetime of a certain definite person. We may here say that the Ordinary of a diocese is empowered to make only the perpetual species of union—the other being reserved to the Holy See.

The Code distinguishes three ways in which benefices may be perpetually or temporarily united: the extinctive union, the equally principal union and the less principal union.

1. *The Extinctive Union*

The extinctive union signifies that from two or more suppressed benefices one new benefice is created, or that two or more benefices are so united that they cease to

24. Santi, *op. cit.*, Tit. V, No. 89.

exist and a new one is created. The benefice which emerges from the union of the two or more obtains the revenue and endowment of the extinct benefices as well as the rights and obligations of both. If these rights and obligations cannot be harmonized the more favorable and desirable are assumed. All extinctive unions are reserved to the Holy See, whether they be perpetual or temporary.

2. *The Equally Principal Union*

The equally principal union signifies that two benefices of the same order or grade are so united that they are in no way changed in nature or status, but that one ecclesiastic obtains both. It is rather a subjective union because the only change effected by the union is that instead of having distinct rectors, the one person rules both without the one benefice being subject to the other. Both churches retain their title and all their rights and ranks as though the union was not made. The most common example of this form of union is in bishoprics. For two or more dioceses and cathedral churches are usually so united that one and the same bishop rules both or all, but each retains its own autonomy.

3. *The Less Principal Union*

The less principal union denotes that an inferior class of benefice or church is united accessorily to a superior benefice in such a fashion that both remain but both are ruled by one rector and the one is subject to the other. The superior church is called the matrix and the inferior the filialis. By this union the title of the inferior benefice or church ceases and it is considered a part of the matrix, and follows the nature of the principal benefice. However, all the obligations of the minor church must be retained. The rector of the principal church becomes the rector of the inferior, and if he cannot personally fulfill the duties he should see that a vicar is appointed to whom a suitable salary is paid. All the rights and privileges of the minor church are retained insofar as they do not conflict with the rights and privileges of the matrix; and in case of conflict the rights and privileges of the matrix prevail.

4. *Unions Reserved to the Holy See*

We have noticed that temporary unions are reserved to the Holy See, as well as all extinctive unions. There are other unions which are not within the power of the Ordinary. For example, the union of two dioceses must be made by Rome. But the most important exception is the union of secular with religious benefices or *vice versa.* Over these unions the Ordinary has no power. Therefore, if a bishop wishes to turn over a parish to a religious order, the change must be made by the Holy See. Ordinaries cannot unite benefices of any kind with the episcopal or capitular table. Once the bishops could make these unions with the consent of the chapters, but on account of the frequency of it, for no other reason than to make the bishops' and chapters' revenue larger, Clement V decreed that bishops could no longer do this, although he did not deny them the power of uniting a certain determined benefice to a certain dignity or canonicate. Finally, bishops are denied the power of uniting benefices outside their diocese, and also those which enjoy the privilege of exemption. The reason is patent; union is an act of jurisdiction and these benefices are not subject to their jurisdiction. Even though the one bishop rules the both dioceses he may not unite two parishes in the different dioceses. It sometimes happens in the United States, for example, at the boundaries of two dioceses, that a church or congregation in one diocese is attended by a priest of another diocese living near the boundaries of the two dioceses, and having "faculties" from both bishops. This union of two congregations of different dioceses could not be criticized before the Code because the congregations were missions rather than parishes or benefices. The law was in force since Trent, but applied only to canonical parishes. Since the Code, however, these unions of parishes cannot be sustained because the status of our parishes has been changed and they are now real canonical parishes and not missions, and canon 1424 very explicitly says that it cannot be done.

5. *Canonical Reasons for Unions*

In uniting benefices a bishop should proceed with the existence and knowledge of a reasonable cause. Cap 33 Tit. V, Lib 111 gives necessity or utility of the Church as sufficient causes, and the Code in canon 1423 repeats the same reasons. Indeed, if a union is made without one of these reasons, it is invalid. For union of benefices must be effected with quite the same solemnity as erection. The juridical status of a benefice cannot be changed except according to law and for the reasons expressed in the law. Unions originated on account of a certain necessity, and necessity is the only excuse for effecting them. The chief reason for uniting two parishes is the poverty of one or both of the parishes. If two or more parishes are too poor to support their own rector, they shuld be united and one rector be given charge of both of them. Another reason given by the authors justifying unions is when the church is in a ruined state and cannot be repaired. Wernz[25] says that the settling of a quarrel is also a sufficient reason to justify a bishop uniting two parishes. Again, scarcity of priests would justify a bishop in uniting two parishes. Therefore, union is rather a matter of necessity than of will.

---

25. *Op. cit.*, Vol. II, No. 27.

6. *Consent of Beneficiaries in Union*

Besides a canonical cause in making a union, the bishop must have the consent of those who actually hold the benefices. He cannot unite two parishes against the will of the rectors. If the possessor is unwilling without a reasonable cause, the bishop can proceed with the union immediately, but the effects of the union will not take place until either the one or the other benefice becomes vacant. Otherwise we should be forced to admit that one benefice was held by two clerics. Trent[26] insinuated this when it decreed that the unions could not be made except without prejudice to those holding the benefices, and canon 1424 repeats this prescription. By common law prior to the Code, the consent of the cathedral chapter was also required, but this the Code has removed. Now, merely the advice of the chapter is needed. This change will not affect the usual procedure in the United States because, while the diocesan consultors perform almost all the duties of the cathedral chapter, nevertheless their consent was never needed by the bishop in order to validate any action. Whenever the consent of the chapter was demanded by common law, the advice of the consultors in the United States was sufficient, according to the Council of Baltimore, which established the consultors in this country to act as the bishop's advisory board in the absence of the cathedral chapters. It need scarcely be remarked that the advice of the consultors cannot be obtained by interviewing them individually; the law specifically requires collegiate action. After hearing their opinion the bishop is free to either accept or reject it, although he is advised not to act contrary to their judgment.

Canon 1428 says that before the Ordinary makes a union he should also hear the interested parties. Trent[27]

---

26. Sess. XXI, c. 5.
27. Sess. XXI, c. 7.

made the same ruling but the authors commenting on it say that, although parishioners are interested parties, still, the failure to call on them and hear their opinion will not invalidate the union. They may indeed have reason to oppose the union, and the older canonists held that they should be given opportunity to express contrary reasons, but not that failure to do so would have any juridical effect. Therefore, in order to avoid useless controversies, it seems right to give them notice of a contemplated union and to hear what they may have to say against the proposed union.

7. *The Union of a Parish With a Religious House*

The union of a parish with a religious house by the Holy See is done in either one of two ways, viz.: in temporals only, or in both temporals and spirituals. Canonists distinguish three possible ways in which a benefice may be united with a monastery or other moral person: *plenissimo jure* and the two above mentioned ways. A union *plenissimo jure* is an *abbatia nullius* or a territory juridically separated from the rest of the diocese, and so does not affect parishes. The union in temporals only is when the corporation becomes the administrator of the temporal revenue of the parish; and a union of both temporal and spiritual matters signifies that the corporation (monastery or university) obtains full possession of the parish.

This union of a benefice with a religious house, called incorporation, had its inception about the ninth century. For the monasteries, founded through the liberality of the faithful, were often given the care of souls of the faithful living in the place. And even churches already established were given them to increase their revenue, and especially after Alexander III had excluded the laity from the possession of churches. In the beginning, incorporation was permitted with the consent of the bishops, but they became too frequent.

This caused the danger of not having enough priests to administer to the people. Consequently, in the Council of Constance,[28] a reformation was decreed, and finally, in Trent,[29] without removing the incorporations already in existence, it wholly interdicted new unions of *parochial* churches with monasteries, abbacies, dignities, cathedral or collegiate churches. Therefore, after Trent, only the Holy See could make these unions, and this law is retained by the Code.

If, then, a parish is united with a religious house in temporals only, the religious house becomes the participant of only the fruits of the parish, and the religious superior should select a secular priest to rule the parish, present him to the Ordinary, and the Ordinary will approve him. This priest is called a perpetual vicar. The religious house is considered as having the parish and is the principal rector, but has only the habitual care of souls. The vicar has the actual care of souls and has a real benefice, because he cannot be removed except for the causes, and in the manner prescribed by law. The habitual pastor cannot interfere with the exercise of the care of souls, as the vicar is the true and properly so-called pastor, since the whole care of souls resides with him independently of the principal pastor, and therefore he exercises it in his own name.[30]

If a parish is united with a religious house in both temporals and spirituals, the superior can name one of his subordinates for the governing of the parish with the approval of the Ordinary. The cleric thus appointed has the actual care of souls and possesses a manual benefice as he can be removed at the will of either the bishop or of his superior, the one without the consent of the other, and without giving the other the reason

---

28. Sess. 43, c. 2.
29. Sess. XXIV, c. 13, de Ref.
30. Canon 471.

for such change.[31] The monastery or other moral person has the habitual care of souls and so the benefice can never become vacant because the moral personality of the monastery cannot die.

In the Third Council of Baltimore,[32] it is required that the bishop have the advice of his consultors before he takes any of the necessary steps toward uniting a parish with a religious house. As this law is not contrary to the Code, it will still continue in force, and the bishop will be required to put the matter before the consultors, although he may act without their consent.

8. *Recourse in Devolutivo to Prevent Unions*

In conclusion we may note that a person has only the right to a recourse in *devolutivo* against the decree of the Ordinary uniting two or more benefices or parishes. Therefore, the order must be obeyed until the Holy See gives a contrary decree. Prior to the Code the Metropolitan could reverse the decision of the Ordinary, but this privilege has been removed by the new law.

On account of the possibility of a recourse to Rome, the bishop should be certain that he has sufficient canonical reason for uniting benefices before he takes the step, because if the opposition can show the contrary, his decree may be nullified by the Holy See. It would be wise for the bishop to state the reasons for union in the decree of union to save himself possible trouble later.

As said above, he may proceed with the union even against the will of the beneficiaries, although the effects will not take place until at least one of the benefices is vacant. The more cautious procedure would be to wait until he obtains a canonical reason for removing or transferring one of the unwilling parties, and then proceed.

---

31. Canon 454, 5.
32. Chap. 2, No. 20.

CHAPTER IV

Other Means of Altering Benefices

1. *The Transfer of a Benefice*

In the preceding chapter we have discussed but one manner of altering a benefice, namely, by union. There remain five other ways in which a benefice may be altered, the first of which is by *transfer*. This may be defined as the change of location of a church or benefice. It takes place, for instance, when a parish church is removed from one part of the parish to another. Not infrequently the location of a church becomes very inconvenient on account of the shifting of the industrial center from one part of the town to another. Again, the value of one section of a city may depreciate and the Catholic population move to another section far removed from the parish church. In such instances it is well for the Ordinary to have the power to change the location of the parish church. The Code gives as the canonical reasons for this change just such causes, namely, great and evident utility or necessity of the Church. He has not, however, any power to change the location of churches belonging to religious orders or congregations as they are in this, as in other things, exempt from his jurisdiction.

The transfer of benefices *other* than parochial can be made by the Ordinary only when the church in which they are founded has collapsed and cannot be restored. In this case they can be transferred to neighboring matrices or to other churches in the same vicinity, and, if possible, special altars or chapels should be erected for them. In the transfer they carry with them all the benefits and obligations of the destroyed church.[33] As in effecting unions, the Ordinary here needs the advice of the consultors and those interested, if there be any.[34]

2. *Division and Dismembration*

The next means of alteration discussed by the Code is by division or dismembration. Division of a benefice is the making of two or more separate benefices from one benefice, while dismembration is the separating part of the territory or of the goods of any benefice and assigning it to another benefice or worthy cause or ecclesiastical institution. Division and dismembration are the most common means of altering benefices. They are to be made when it becomes evident that the beneficiary cannot satisfy all his obligations, and this happens when the parish church is too far distant from some of the parishioners, or when there are too many parishioners so that the pastor cannot administer to them even with the aid of assistants.

It is certain that before Trent the bishops could of their own will divide parishes. But from Chapter 4, Sess. XXI, *De Ref.*, it became necessary to look for the two above reasons before proceeding. If the great number of parishioners could be attended with the aid of assistants, the pastor was commanded by the constitution "*Apostolici Ministerii*" of Innocent XIII to take as many assistants as necessary and present them to the bishop for examination and confirmation. This was the common law, but in France and other places the assistants were named by the bishop and were removed by the bishops without consulting the pastors. This happened also in this country. De Angelis[35] says that this condition of affairs resulted from the peculiar manner

33. Canon 1426.
34. Canon 1428.
35. Tit. V, Lib. III.

of administration in those places, namely, that the bishop had the exclusive right of providing the cleric with a title of ordination and of providing him with support until he gave him a duty to perform. Since the Code the bishops have this right of selecting the assistants of the pastor and appointing them after hearing the opinion of the pastor. Hence, what was exceptional before the Code is now made common law. But it is to be noticed that the assistant is appointed only after the pastor is heard; so that if the pastor is not consulted the appointment of the assistant is not valid. This fact will have its importance in certain parochial functions which are not to the point here.

It is likewise the right of the bishop to determine the number of assistants so that if the pastor does not designate enough the bishop can compel him to it. In the supposition that the church was too far removed from some of the parishioners, Trent gave the bishops the faculty of erecting a new parish even when the pastor was unwilling. The law wished the pastor to be heard, but if he be unreasonably unwilling, the bishop could proceed with the division against his wishes. Such was the law of Trent, although looking at the decisions of the Congregation of the Council, to which were brought the cases of division of parishes, sometimes the division was permitted on account of the too great multitude of parishioners, and other times denied on account of the too great distance from the parochial church of the faithful. The Code has now reiterated the law of Trent so that the two reasons for dividing a parish are too great distance from some of the parishioners, and too great multitude of people to be taken care of by the pastor even with the aid of assistants. If the Holy See reverses any decreed of division in the future it will be because it considers that neither of these canonical reasons are present.

Therefore, as in the case of union, the bishop should

first determine whether or not he can prove his reasons before proceeding with the division, and as a precautionary measure he should incorporate them into the decree of division. The bishop must hear the opinion of the consultors and of the pastors involved, and also of other interested parties, but can make the division against the judgment of all of these if he so desires. The Code demands that the division be made by an authentic document but this does not affect the validity, just as it does not affect validity in transfer, unions and the like.

The Congregation of the Council sometimes decreed that instead of a new parish, a perpetual vicariate should be erected in the parish, and the Code allows this also, when, in the opinion of the bishop, it is the most suitable way to settle the difficulty. In this case the vicar should be assigned a suitable salary. In making a new parish or perpetual vicariate, the Ordinary should see that there is suitable revenue for both the divided parish and the new entity, dividing up the resources and the debts in just proportion. If the mother church has only enough for her own support the parishioners should provide for the new parish.

When the Holy See divides a parish belonging to a religious community, the newly-formed parish or perpetual vicariate is secular.[36] Although canon 1427 says that for a just and canonical reason the Ordinary may divide *any* parishes, nevertheless parishes belonging to religious are not included in this, as can be seen in canon 1422, where it is plainly stated that the division or dismembration of any religious parish is reserved to the Holy See. Therefore, 1427 must be interpreted in the light of 1422 and the ordinary doctrine deduced, namely, that the Ordinary has no power over exempt parishes.

Dismembration is merely another way of settling

---

36. Canon 1428, 1.

the difficulty when a pastor has too many parishioners, or when part of his parish is too far removed from the parish church. The territory is then assigned to another already existing parish. The formalities, reasons and the rest are exactly the same for dismembration as for division. Canon 1422 tells us that the Ordinary cannot dismember a benefice in this fashion, namely, that the goods are taken away from it without erecting a new benefice. At first sight this seems to prevent the Ordinary from dismembering parishes because in this supposition the parish goods are taken away from it and given to another parish but no new benefice is erected. However, canon 1427 tells us expressly that the Ordinary has this power. Therefore, we must understand canon 1422 as a general rule for all benefices, while canon 1427 is to be taken as an exception for parochial benefices.

After legislating concerning dismembration, the Code gives some rules on *pensions* which are quasi-dismembrations insofar as they denote the separation of part of the goods of the benefice in favor of some cleric other than the beneficiary. Pensions are two-fold: *perpetual* and *temporary.* A perpetual pension is that part of the revenue of a benefice separated perpetually from the benefice and given to a cleric for the performance of some office, or for some other person. When the pensionary dies, another cleric obtains the pension. Temporary pensions are sub-divided into two classes, namely, those which perdure during the life of the pensionary, whether or not the beneficiary outlives him, and those which last only during the life of the beneficiary. The authors call the first two kinds of pension real pensions, or in other words, pensions which are attached to the benefice itself; while the last kind is a personal pension adhering not to the benefice, but to the person of the beneficiary.

As noted above, canon 1422 denies to Ordinaries the right to separate part of the goods of a benefice without erecting a new benefice, and we have seen one exception with regard to parochial benefices treated in canon 1427. With regard to temporary personal pensions, the rule of canon 1422 suffers another exception. The Ordinary is empowered by canon 1429 to grant to a cleric, for a just reason, a pension to last during the life, not of the pensionary, but of the beneficiary, provided the Ordinary makes the grant at the time of appoinment to the benefice, and expresses it in the actual decree of appointment. It is supposed that a sufficient amount of revenue is reserved for the beneficiary, otherwise the pension cannot be imposed.

The Ordinary can impose a pension on a *parochial* benefice only in favor of the pastor or vicar when they are leaving office; but pensions can be imposed on other forms of benefices in favor of other persons for any just reason. The pension imposed on a parochial benefice cannot exceed one-third of the total amount of revenue after the uncertain revenue and expenses have been deducted. This holds regardless of how large the revenue of the parish may be. Pensions on other forms of benefices have no limit save that a suitable portion be reserved for the beneficiary, and the Ordinary is the judge in the matter. Pensions granted by the Holy Father or by other inferior prelates cease with the death of the pensionary, if he dies before the beneficiary, and they cannot be alienated except this has been expressly granted.

Before the Code it was a disputed question among the authors whether or not bishops could impose a pension on a parochial benefice. Trent[37] allowed bishops to do it, but a later decree of Innocent XII given 11 Nov., 1692, and approved by Benedict XIII, 24 Sept., 1724, "*Quanta Pastoribus,*" forbade Ordinaries to impose pensions on any parochial churches. Some authors

---

37. Sess. XXIV, c. 3, De Ref.

therefore contended that the temporary personal pension was imposed, not on the benefice, but on the person of the beneficiary, and so could be imposed with the consent of the beneficiary. The action of the Holy See in granting indults to Ordinaries to impose pensions, seems to indicate that it was forbidden by common law. Cfr. Faculty given the bishops of Canada to assign pensions to pastors or missionaries resigning their parishes or mssions on account of sickness, provided they labored there for ten years.[38] In this country it is customary for the bishop to form a society in his diocese for the support of infirm or old priests, and this obviates any necessity for pensions.

3. *Conversion of a Benefice*

The last method to be considered here for the altering of a benefice is the *conversion* into another state. Conversion may be defined as the changing of the nature of a benefice into something different, for example, the making of a simple benefice into a parochial church, or the making of an episcopal church into the metropolitan church. The power of the Ordinary is limited to the conversion of benefices not having the care of souls into benefices with the care of souls, but not *vice versa.* He may not change a secular benefice into a religious, nor a religious into a secular benefice. This power the Ordinary had, without any of it being changed by the Code; nor can we find any difficulty in the case given by Garcia, p. XII, "*De Benef.*," that simple benefices cannot be converted into curata by the Ordinary. For, as he himself says, we must understand this to mean that the Ordinary cannot do this without cause, that is, without utility or necessity of the Church. The Code does not say that the conversion will be invalid if done without these reasons prompting it, as it does say with

38. Putzer, *op. cit.*, 1898, No. 249.

regard to union, transfer, division and dismembration. Therefore, if done without strict canonical cause, it will be valid, provided the Ordinary have at least some good reason for making the change.

The final method given by the Code for altering a benefice is by *suppression,* but as this is reserved to the Holy See, it offers no difficulty to the Ordinaries. Sebastianelli[39] says that as it is the total extinction of a benefice, and lessens worship, it is to be considered odious in law, but that nevertheless the bishop may, with the consent of the cathedral chapter, suppress a benefice for a just cause. The Code now says that all acts of suppression are reserved to the Holy See and thereby takes it out of the hands of the Ordinary in all cases.

---

39. *Op. cit.,* "*De Rebus,*" No. 333, page 327.

CHAPTER V

Appointment to Benefices

1. *General Notions*

An ecclesiastical benefice cannot be obtained without canonical appointment,[40] so that anyone who takes a benefice without canonical appointment is an intruder and is, *ipso facto,* deprived of any presumptive right he may have had to it, besides being liable to heavy punishments mentioned in the law. Under the name canonical appointment come both the free disposition and the necessary disposition of benefices. Here we treat only of the free disposition because all the benefices in this country are at the free disposal of the bishops. Necessary disposition is that appointing in which the bishop has no choice, but must appoint a cleric chosen by some other person, for example, the patron of a benefice.

Prescinding from some particular law or concordat by which the Pope gives to some other person the right to make the selection of a beneficiary for a vacant benefice, the power of appointing the cleric ordinarily belongs to the Pope for the whole Church, and to the bishop in his territory. To the Pope this belongs because of his supreme, full, absolute and immediate jurisdiction over each and every one of the faithful and over every pastor and his church. For the first twelve centuries the Pope never or rarely gave out benefices in the diocese of his bishops, since the appointment of the benefice and the ordination of the cleric were considered inseparable. But after the twelfth century the separation was made between conferring Orders and obtaining a benefice, and

40. Canon 147.

the Popes, either to provide the necessary means of support for clerics who had been ordained without a title by the bishops against the canons, or to provide for the welfare of certain men who had merited well of the Church, gave out benefices vacant in the Church, or even granted to them the right to certain benefices when they became vacant in the future. This was done either by commands called "*mandata de providendo*" or by letters called "*litterae expectativae.*"

The *mandata de providendo* were letters sent by the Pope to the bishop recommending a certain cleric for a benefice vacant in the diocese of the bishop. The bishop could reject these *mandata* for a good reason to be explained afterwards to the Pope, but without the good reason they could not refuse to execute them; if they did refuse, they were admonished, and then declared contumacious, and the execution of the mandata was given to another prelate who first declared the appointment made by the bishop to be null. The *litterae expectativae* were Apostolic letters given to bishops in favor of certain clergy in regard to a benefice not yet vacant, whether it was a particular benefice, or merely the first one to become vacant. These letters of the Popes were fundamentally just and proper, but on account of their frequency, caused many abuses. They lessened the power of the bishops, and often through false allegations made to the Pope, the less fitted were appointed to benefices. Indeed, some unscrupulous clergy, after having obtained these letters from the Pope, sold them to the highest bidder. The abuses were so great that Trent[41] decreed that they could not thereafter be given, and Pius V, in his constitution, "*Sacrosanctum,*" on 9th of Sept., 1568, confirmed this. It was not the intention of Trent to limit the power of the Pope, but merely to meet the subterfuges of inferior clerics, and

41. Sess. XXIV, c. 19.

since Trent the Popes have conferred benefices in the dioceses of bishops through reservations.

2. *Reservation of Benefices*

A *reservation* is the act of removing from the jurisdiction of the bishop the conferring of a benefice to become vacant in the future. When reservations first came into practice there arose great controversies as to the power of the bishops and the Pope. Some alleged that the bishops were merely the quasi-vicars of the Pope; others claimed that the bishop had the exclusive right to confer benefices in his diocese, denying the power of the Pope to exercise jurisdiction in the dioceses of bishops. The controversy was settled by certain rules whereby certain benefices were reserved to the Pope, while others were given to the bishop for appointment.

In particular cases, however, the Pope may confer any benefice regardless of whether or not it is usually reserved by common law or custom. For we cannot deny the right to the Pope to confer a benefice on a cleric in the diocese of a bishop, especially when it is necessary to limit any excess of bishops. On the other hand, the power of bishops must not be regarded as vicariate power of the Pope, for they are the true leaders, and among other rights have the right of administration which includes the appointing to benefices. Nor must we admit that it is the ordinary thing for the Pope to confer benefices in dioceses, for the bishops are placed there by the Holy Ghost to rule the dioceses, and among their ordinary powers is this power of conferring benefices. This is seen from the history of benefices, for when the conferring of a benefice was not distinguished from the conferring of Holy Orders, to confer Orders presupposed the conferring of a benefice. But nobody denies the right of bishops to confer Orders on their subjects. Nor is it evident that this right of appointment to benefices was ever taken away from the bishops in the history of the Church.

3. *Reservations Specified in the Code*

Reservations are odious in the law, and therefore are of strict interpretation. In doubt, the power of the bishop must always be sustained until it is clear that the Pope has actually reserved the particular benefice.

The parochial benefices reserved by common law to the Holy See are:

1. Those becoming vacant by the death, promotion, resignation or transfer of the familiares of the Pope, even those who are familiares only honorarily. This would seem to indicate that parochial benefices held by monsignors are reserved to the Pope when they become vacant in the manner stated.

2. Those benefices founded outside of the Roman Curia, when the vacancy occurs by death of the beneficiary in Rome. Before the Code it was considered that manual benefices, both secular and religious, were exempt from this reservation.[42] Now it is clear that manual benefices are not included, but manual benefices are restricted to religious benefices; all secular benefices being perpetual.

The above two reservations are repetitions of the old law, and consequently must be interpreted same as the old law on the subject, the interpretation given by the authors is that the reservation lasts for a month from the day of vacancy. If the Pope does not fill them within the month, the ordinary prelate to make the appointment is free to proceed with the filling of the benefice.

3. Those benefices invalidly conferred on account of simony. Canon 729 says that if simony has been committed with regard to benefices, any following ap-

---

42. Bouix, *De Parocho*, page 319.

pointment is null even though the simony was done by a third party, whether with or without the knowledge of the person concerned, as long as it was not done to defraud him or against his will. The person is further commanded to return the thing simoniacally exchanged, if it be possible, and give up the benefice before any trial is held in the matter; and may not make the revenue of the benefice his own. If he has made some revenue his own in good faith, it is left to the prudent judgment of the Ordinary to decide whether or not he may be allowed or keep part or all of it.

Canon 1441 tells us that deductions from the revenues, compensations or payments made by the cleric in the act of receiving a benefice in favor of the person appointing, or of the patron or other person, are to be considered as simoniacal. The old canons condemned these, as also did Trent,[43] reprobating all customs even immemorial to this effect. The constitutions of S. Pius V, "*Nimis durum,*" of 31 May, 1750, and of Innocent XII, "*Ecclesiae,*" of 22 Sept., 1695, and many decrees of the Sacred Congregation of the Council, may be added to this decree of Trent. Looking well at these documents, only those payments made in the act of provision must be condemned which go to the person giving the benefice, or to the patron or others, but not those payments which are to be applied to the building of the church, or another holy place, provided this reservation of funds is made without any agreement with the person on whom the benefice is conferred.

When, therefore, a benefice has been given simoniacally, the appointment is invalid, and the benefice becomes reserved to the Pope, so that the bishop has no power to confer it.

4. Those benefices which the Roman Pontiff, either personally or by his delegate, "lays his hands on," either

43. Sess. XXIV, c. 14, de ref.

by declaring the election to the benefice void, or by forbidding electors to proceed; or if he accepts the resignation of the beneficiary, or if he promotes, transfers or deprives him; and also those benefices which he gives *in commendam.*

This "laying of hands" on a benefice is closely allied to reservation. It may be called a tacit reservation made by the Pope on the disposition of a particular benefice, by reason of which the ordinary prelate to confer it cannot make the appointment for that particular time. It differs from reservation, first, because reservation is brought about by common law or by decree, the other by a fact; secondly, the reservation of a benefice is perpetual or until the Pope dies, according as how it was reserved, while the laying on of hands by the Pope affects the disposition of the benefice for that time only. It was first introduced in Cap. 2, Tit. II, Lib. III, Extra comm., in which chapter was settled a question concerning the officials of the Roman Curia, namely, whether or not they were reserved after the death of the Pope. We must note that it is not any laying on of hands by the Pope, but only that act by which the Pope, with certain knowledge, intends to reserve the appointment of the benefice. Like reservation, it is odious in the law, and therefore of strict interpretation. Wherefore, in doubt, the bishop may exercise his right until the contrary becomes evident to him. According to the rule we are here considering, the benefice of a cleric who is promoted by the Pope, is reserved. An example of this would be when a pastor is made a bishop. The conferring of his parish is for that time reserved to the Pope. The four rules thus far discussed are found in canon 1435.

5. Those benefices which the Ordinary of the diocese fails to fill within six months after he knows of its vacancy, unless the circumstances of place and persons persuade him to defer the appointment beyond six

months.[44] The reservations in numbers one and two are perpetual, but if the Pope does not appoint the beneficiary within a month, the ordinary prelate may make the selection. The reservations in numbers three, four and five are applicable to only the one occasion and are not perpetually reserved to the Pope. However, in the last named cases, the Ordinary has no power to act, regardless of whether or not the Pope delays longer than a month.

4. *Necessity of Benefice Being Vacant*

So much for the power of the Pope to confer benefices in the dioceses of bishops. We have said that the bishop is the ordinary person to make the appointments. He has what is called the "intention founded in the law," which means that whoever else makes the claim to this right must prove it. This principal is valid against any alleged right of a patron or other person to name the beneficiary of a vacant benefice. In making appointments the bishop must be careful to observe the rules prescribed by the canons, and especially the law of 1432, which says that he can confer only vacant benefices. No promise of a benefice not yet vacant has any juridical value, according to canon 150. In this matter he differs from the Pope, who is above the canon law, and need observe only those things which are of divine precept with regard to appointments.

A benefice is vacant *de jure* only, or *de facto* only, or both *de jure* and *de facto*. It is vacant *de jure* only, when nobody possesses the title to it, although somebody has possession of it. It is vacant *de facto* only, when someone has obtained the title to it but has not yet taken possession of it or was put out of it so that now the benefice has no possessor. Lastly it is vacant *de jure* and *de facto*, when nobody has the title to it and nobody

---

44. 1432, 3.

possesses it. The bishop may confer a benefice which is both *de jure* and *de facto* vacant. A benefice which is only *de jure* vacant can also be given out by the bishop, but in this case he must see whether the person possessing has a colored title or not. If he has a colored title, he must be summoned and his title taken away from him; if he has no title the bishop need not delay the appointment of the future beneficiary, but the person in possession must be summoned before the bishop before the bishop sends the second cleric to take possession. Benefices which are vacant neither *de jure* nor *de jure* and *de facto* cannot be filled by the bishop, as is evident.

Since bishops cannot confer benefices not yet vacant, a word may be said about coadjutors. A coadjutor is a cleric appointed by competent authority to help a beneficiary perform his duties. He is either permanent or temporary, either has the right to succession or has not the right. The usual example of permanent coadjutors is with regard to bishoprics, while the usual place to find temporary coadjutors is in parishes. A legitimate reason for appointing a coadjutor is old age on the part of the beneficiary, or insanity, incapability, blindness or other permanent disability in the beneficiary, or when there is too much work for him to do. From the very idea of coadjutors it is clear that a permanent coadjutor with right of succession can be made only by the Holy See for it filling of a benefice not yet vacant. This is the law of the Decretals, Cap. 2, Tit. VIII, Lib. III, and other places, and of Trent,[45] and also the law of the Code.[46] As to temporary coadjutors, we must distinguish between consistorial and non-consistorial benefices. It is patent that only the Pope can give a coadjutor to a consistorial benefice, as he is the only prelate having jurisdiction over consistorial benefices. As

45. Sess. XXV, c. 7, de Ref.
46. Canon 1433.

to inferior benefices, bishops have the faculty to grant coadjutors for the canonical reasons mentioned above.[47]

The coadjutor with or without future succession should have the same qualities as the beneficiary, and is to be assigned a suitable portion of the revenue of the benefice. It is presumed that there is enough revenue for both the beneficiary and the coadjutor, otherwise the beneficiary has the first right and the coadjutor must be supported in some other way according as the bishop directs.[48]

5. *The Term "Ordinary" in Appointment to Benefices*

Before giving the particular rules which must guide the Ordinary in the distribution of benefices, we must note that, although the term "Ordinary" in the Code usually includes the vicar general, in this matter of conferring benefices the vicar general is expressly excepted unless he has a special mandate from the bishop.[49] This prevents any conflict of authority in the appointing of pastors, and assures harmony of action in the diocese. As the Code requires a *special* mandate, the bishop cannot validly give the vicar general a general mandate for all appointments, but only a special mandate for the particular cases.

When the diocese is vacant, the vicar of the chapter, or the administrator (as is the case in this country), has no power of appointment until the diocese is vacant a year. After a year he may fill any benefices of free collation, that is, those whose appointment depends on the wish of the bishop, when they become vacant. This in an innovation; hitherto the vicar or administrator required the permission of the Holy See to confer any vacant benefices regardless of how long the See was vacant.[50]

---

47. 475, 476, 350.
48. Trent Sess. XXI, c. 6, de Re.
49. Canon 1432, 2.
50. Wernz, *op. cit.*, Vol II, No. 339.

CHAPTER VI

Rules for Appointment to Benefices

1. *Consent of Beneficiary*

The first rule given by the Code[51] is that an ecclesiastical benefice cannot be validly conferred on an unwilling cleric, nor a cleric not expressly accepting the appointment. This is simply a repetition of a law found in the *Corpus Juris*.[52] In the United States the clergy are ordained under the title either of mission work, or of the service of the Church, and therefore should accept any charge given them by their bishop. If they be unreasonably unwilling, therefore, they may be punished by the bishop.

We shall see later that a man possessing a removable parochial benefice may be transferred against his will to another benefice of about the same grade. He is given this second benefice against his will and this, therefore, seems to constitute an exception to the above rule. We will discuss the history and reason for this later when we treat of the transfer of pastors.

Nobody can confer a benefice on himself.[53] This prohibition is similar to the one recorded in canon 170, which says that nobody can validly vote for himself. The bishop, therefore, cannot acquire for himself any of the vacant benefices in his diocese. Nor can the administrator, during a vacancy of the See, appoint himself to a benefice becoming vacant, even though he would prob-

---

51. Canon 1436.
52. C. 17, III, 4 in Sexto.
53. 1437.

ably be appointed to it, on account of his seniority, by the bishop, were the See not vacant.

2. *Appointment Must be Perpetual*

All secular benefices must be conferred for life unless the law of foundation of the benefice, or a particular indult, or an immemorial custom permit otherwise.[54] We have noticed above that all secular parochial benefices are perpetual whether the pastor be removable or irremovable, because these terms simply designate the procedure to be followed in his transfer or removal. Benefices are conferred for life, and when necessity arises the law allows the bishop to promote the welfare of his diocese by transferring or removing these perpetual beneficiaries. But this must be done only for reasons expressed in the law; so that they are really perpetual and can be removed only when necessity, which is supposed to know no law, demands.

The contrary of the above rule is true with regard to religious pastors as they are all removable at the will of either the bishop or their religious superior.[55] The reason for not making a religious pastor permanent is that they are bound by vow of obedience to their superior to go wherever he may send them, and the obtaining of a permanent benefice would seriously endanger the operation of such a vow.

Since the origin of benefices this subjective perpetuity has been considered an essential quality until the publication of the Code when manual benefices were first officially recognized as true and real benefices. It is true that prior to the Code many of the authors considered manual benefices as canonical in favorable things, and even some went so far as to suggest that they were real benefices. But it has always been against

54. 1438.
55. 454, 5.

the idea of a benefice to have the beneficiary removable. At the time of the Council of Trent parishes were not everywhere erected and the Council[56] decreed that wherever parish churches had not definite limits nor a particular rector, the bishops should assign a distinct population as a certain and particular parish with its own particular and *perpetual* rector or *provide in some more useful manner* as the circumstances of the place demanded. This was a distinct departure from the common law regarding the creation of parishes and was the reason why parishes were not everywhere created in the fashion approved by the Church. The removable species of canonical parishes in France after the Revolution, was another departure, because it recognized as canonical, parishes which were subjectively temporary. Although this was by way of toleration on account of conditions, nevertheless it created a new custom on the subject. The *Maxima Cura* in 1910 abolished this removable *ad nutum* form of canonical parish and made all parishes subjectively perpetual, as was always the desire of the Church.[57] And now the Code, while renewing the prescriptions of the *Maxima Cura,* with regard to the subjective perpetuity of secular pastors, has provided for the needs of such places as were formerly under the direction of the Congregation of the Propaganda, by declaring that while they remain perpetual, nevertheless some are more stable than others, and divides them into the removable and the irremovable pastors, a distinction which is entirely new with the Code. The condition, therefore, which gave rise to the division of the missions of the United States into removable and irremovable rectorships has been provided for now that the Code has caused them to be canonical parishes and it will not be difficult to apply the law of tenure to the pastors for that very reason.

56. Sess. XXIV, c. 8, de Ref.
57. Bargilliat, "*Praelectiones Juris Canonici,*" Vol. II, No. 1011, 1915.

The rule under consideration says that all secular benefices are perpetual unless an immemorial custom permits otherwise. Some may claim that here is an immemorial custom in favor of the removable *ad nutum* parishes, but it does not seem that any such custom may be alleged. In its missionary state this country had no parishes, and therefore no custom could have originated with regard to canonical parishes. Our parishes are in a new state and any custom that is to exist must arise in the future. The rule says that a particular indult may permit secular benefices to be conferred otherwise than subjectively perpetual. An example of this was the indult obtained by the Plenary Council of Latin America in 1899 to appoint canonical pastors with a revokable *ad nutum* title.[58]

The law of foundation may also provide that the pastor be removable *ad nutum*. Canon 1417 provides that in the founding of a benefice, the founder may, with the consent of the Ordinary, place conditions which are contrary to the common law, provided they are honorable and not contrary to the nature of benefices. To place such a condition on the subjective tenure would therefore be allowed, and once admitted, would compel the Ordinary to give such benefice with a revokable title.

3. *Plurality of Benefices*

No cleric is capable of accepting and retaining, either in title or *in commendam*, a plurality of incompatible benefices as defined by canon 156, which says that those benefices are incompatible, which cannot be simultaneously fulfilled by the beneficiary. Moreover, those benefices are incompatible, of which one alone is sufficient for the decent support of the cleric obtaining it.[59]

In the beginning of benefices, when there was made no distinction between residential and non-residential

58. Wernz, *op. cit.*, Vol. II, No. 823.
59. 1439.

benefices, it was unheard of that one cleric should possess more than one benefice. After the distinction came into use clerics began to acquire two or more benefices, often without any other reason than to increase their revenue. As the one man could not be in two or three places at the same time, some of the benefices were without a rector for long spaces of time, the rector was given occasion to do much traveling, and many other abuses were common. Each church not having its own resident pastor was without a defender in times of need and churches were allowed to go to ruin. Again, the one person could not properly attend to all the people and the spiritual side of the office was often neglected. It was, therefore, highly proper for Trent[60] to return to the discipline of the *Corpus Juris* that each benefice should be given to a particular person and that a plurality should not be conferred on any one cleric.[61] We have already, in the first chapter, treated the question of when a plurality may be admitted by the Ordinary.

When a cleric, therefore, receives and accepts an office incompatible with the one which he already possesses, he is considered as having resigned the first office and in law it is vacant, according to canon 188, 3. If he presumes to hold the first benefice after having obtained possession of the second, he is deprived of both by the law itself, according to canon 2396. Schmalzgrueber[62] says that according to the law of Trent (of which the Code law is merely a repetition), anyone who has obtained two incompatible benefices, although he is deprived of both of them by law, nevertheless is not bound to leave both of them at the same time; the difference being that he may hold the second benefice until a declaratory sentence has been given. For although

60. Sess. XXIV, c. 17, de Ref.
61. Chapter 1, 2, Cause 21, q. 1; Chap. 5, 13, Tit. V, Lib. III; Chap. 23, Tit. IV, Lib. III in VI.
62. Schmalzgrueber, Vol. 12, page 285. *"Jus Canonicum Universum,"* Parisiis, 1864-1867.

he has lost the title, he may retain possession until he has been declared deprived of it. As we are to retain the same interpretation where the law remains the same, we may hold the opinion of this author. But the bishop should institute proceedings against such a cleric so that he may be removed from it in punishment of his presumption, as the law directs.

At one time the Ordinaries had the faculty to confer incompatible benefices but since clerics obtained from them the necessary dispensation without really grave causes, the faculty was taken away from Ordinaries, and now only the Holy See grants the permission.[63] According to a declaration of the Sacred Congregation of the Council, 14 August, 1632, the reasons which will prompt the Holy See to make such exception are either necessity or utility of the Church, or the great merits of the Man. Whatever be the reason for asking this favor, the grant is null unless mention is made of the fact that he has a benefice.[64] If the cleric, after having obtained such a dispensation, afterwards resigns the second benefice, he may not again assume it without a new dispensation, for the dispensation being contrary to common law, must be interpreted strictly, and hence does not revive.

4. *Benefices to be Conferred Without Diminution*

Ecclesiastical benefices should be given without diminution except those allowed by canon 1429, 1, 2, the substance of which is that for a just reason the Ordinary may impose a temporary pension for the life of the beneficiary, provided there is sufficient revenue allowed to the beneficiary; but for parochial benefices the only pension allowed is one in favor of a retiring pastor or vicar of the benefice.[65] Diminution may be defined as

63. Sebastianelli, *op. cit.*, De Rebus, No. 245.
64. Cap. 21, Tit. IV, Lib. III in VI; Canon 156.
65. 1440.

an innovation, on the occasion of appointment, on account of which the benefice is less desirable or which makes the obligations of the beneficiary heavier.

Canonists distinguish three kinds of diminution: first, the imposition of obligations which are not included in the decree of foundation of the benefice; secondly, the payment by the appointee of anything on the occasion of his appointment; and lastly, the separation of part of the fruit or revenues of the benefice when conferring it.

The first sort of diminution was condemned by Trent[66] in the following words: "Reason demands that from those things which are well constituted nothing be subtracted by contrary laws. When, therefore, certain qualities are required, or certain burdens are imposed, by the erection or foundation of any benefice, or by other constitutions, they should not be derogated from in any appointment to the benefice, or in any other disposition of it."

The second kind of diminution regards the payment of something when the benefice is being conferred. When treating of reservations brought about through simony we said that, according to canon 1441, deductions from the revenues, or payments or compensations made by the cleric in the act of receiving a benefice, are forbidden when made in favor of the patron, but not when made in favor of the building or another place, provided this reservation of funds is made without an agreement with the person on whom the benefice is conferred. The question can be raised here with regard to annates or that part of the fruits of a benefice, which is given to the Holy See when the benefice is conferred by the Holy See. Canon 1482 says that where this practice is in vogue it should be retained, and that all laudable customs and statutes prevailing in any region with regard

66. Sess. XXV, c. 5, de Ref.

to this matter should be preserved. The payments thus made to the Holy See are used for the support of the Holy Father, the cardinals and nuncios, and for the propagation of the faith, and it has been officially declared in the Council of Constance that these payments cannot be considered simoniacal. The law of annates has never been introduced into this county and has, therefore, no importance for us.

Enforcing the law of canon 1441 with regard to payments made on the occasion of receiving a benefice, the bishops should diligently inspect the constitutions and customs in vogue, and approve only those which they think praiseworthy; the rest they should abolish as scandalous, as directed by Trent.[67]

The third form of diminution takes place when part of the fruits of the benefice are separated in some permanent way, while the same obligations remain. The usual manner of doing this is by the imposition of pensions, and the rule under consideration, given in canon 1440, makes allowance for certain kinds of pensions, the nature of which we have already seen above. Any other kinds of pensions are forbidden without the express consent of the Holy See.

5. *Appointment to Secular and Religious Benefices.*

Secular benefices must be conferred only on secular clergy; religious benefices must be given to the members of the order to which the benefice belongs.[68] We find this rule in the *Corpus,* Cap. 5, Tit. VI, Lib. 1, and other places, and also in Trent.[69] With regard to parochial benefices, it is clear that they are, by their nature, secular, because the very purpose of a religious order is something other than the care of souls in parishes. The natural and ordinary procedure is that the care of

67. Sess. XXIV, c. 14, de Ref.
68. Canon 1442.
69. Sess. XIV, c. 10, de Ref.

souls is entrusted to the bishop and his secular priests. In the beginning the bishop was the only person in the diocese who had the responsibility for this work and he surrounded himself with priests to help him in the accomplishment of the task. Later on the dioceses were divided up into parishes and the bishop was instructed to appoint priests in the districts called parishes. The history of religious orders shows us that they had their origin on account of some pressing need of the times other than parochial duty, for instance, to teach the young; or for the purpose of leading the contemplative life.

Secular benefices must, therefore, according to the canon, be given to the members of the secular clergy. When it is advisable to place a religious priest in charge of a secular benefice, the Holy See or the bishop makes him merely the administrator and the benefice remains secular. When a parish is united only in temporals to a monastery or religious house, it remains secular and should be ruled over by a secular priest.

The second part of the rule is not so clear as the first; namely, that all religious benefices should be given to the members of the religious order or institute to which the benefice belongs. It is clear enough that the superior may not appoint a member of an order other than his own. But may he appoint a secular priest? Canon 1425, 2, says that when a parish is united *pleno jure,* that is, in both temporals and spirituals, with a religious house, the superior *may* name one of his subjects to take active charge of it. The wording of the canon does not seem to indicate that he must name a religious of his community, but that he is free to name a secular vicar just as he is required to do when the parish is united in temporals only. Canon 456, on the other hand, instructs the religious superior to present to the Ordinary for confirmation a priest of his own order to rule a parish given to his order. Therefore, after a comparison of canons 1425, 2, and 456, it seems probable that the rule under consideration should be understood to mean that the religious superior should not appoint a secular to rule any of the parishes entrusted to the care of the order.

6. *Procedure for Installation to a Benefice*

Nobody may, of his own authority, take possession of a benefice which has been conferred on him; nor may he take possession of it before he has made the profession of faith if it be one of those benefices for which the profession is prescribed.[70]

Every appointment to a benefice includes three things, namely, the selection of the person, the conferring on him of the benefice, and lastly the installation or giving him the possession of it. An ecclesiastic, though appointed to a benefice, cannot take possession of it of his own authority, but must be installed by the bishop or by someone designated by the bishop. The purpose of this ceremony is to avoid confusion or any doubt about the person of the newly appointed beneficiary. It is of strict obligation to observe the laws with regard to this installation as can be seen from canon 2394, which legislates that anyone who obtains possession of a benefice of his own authority is by law rendered incapable of the office, and moreover is to be punished according to the gravity of his fault by the Ordinary; and if he does not leave the benefice he is to be compelled by suspension, privation of any benefice or office he already holds, and even by deposition.

The law itself contains no prescribed form for this installation and therefore the prescriptions of local laws, or the local customs with regard to this matter, must be followed. In the United States there were, as a rule, no formalities observed when a rector took office before the

70. 1443.

publication of the Code. It was not strictly required on account of the absence of parishes, but in the future a man must be installed unless the Ordinary dispenses from it in writing; in which case the dispensation will take the place of installation.[71]

In the time of the Decretals it was the privilege of the archdeacon to make the installation, but after archdeacons lost their jurisdiction it became the right of the Ordinary to do it. He may do it personally or through some other ecclesiastic, as, for instance, his vicar general. The person to be installed also has the option of either receiving it personally or through a procurator to whom he has given a special *mandata*.[72]

Canon 1444, 2, directs the Ordinary to define the time within which the installation must take place; when this time is passed without the cleric having become invested, the Ordinary is to declare the benefice vacant, unless there be a just impediment preventing the cleric from acting.

The effects of canonical possession are chiefly:

1. The beneficiary makes the fruits of the benefice his own from the time of the installation.[73]

2. He is assured the possession of the benefice if, after a space of three years, it be discovered that he had not a legitimate title. Canon 1446 says that a cleric who possesses a benefice and proves that for three years he has been in peaceful possession of it in good faith, although with an invalid title, obtains the legitimate title by prescription, provided there was no simony. It is to be noted here that some title is required, as the canon makes mention of a title, even though it be invalid. The peaceful possession mentioned by the Code does not signify that nobody has contested the benefice for three years, but that he has been in possession and that any-

71. Canon 1444.
72. Canon 1445.
73. Canon 1472.

body that perchance may have disputed his right to the benefice, has been given a contrary judgment by the court.[74]

3. A cleric thus installed cannot be deposed by another claimant without a definite sentence in a petitory trial. Canon 1447 says that whoever demands a benefice peacefully possessed by another, and who claims that the benefice is canonically vacant, must give, in the petition, the name of the possessor, the time of his possession and the special reason alleged for the vacancy; but the benefice cannot be given to the plaintiff until the case has been decided in a petitory action. This is, in substance, the same as the law preceding the Code, which is found in the 35th rule of the Apostolic Chancery; differing, however, in this: that the 35th rule applied only to benefices which were peacefully possessed for a *year;* now it applied to all benefices legitimately possessed regardless of the length of time except that it be under three years.

4. The installation into a benefice also causes a benefice formerly held by the person to become vacant when the former is incompatible.[75] The law here provides that although a beneficiary obtain a new benefice, he may retain the old one until he has actually taken possession of the second, and thus is never without the title to some benefice. It provides for the automatical vacancy of the first benefice and prevents any serious trouble later concerning the resignation of the cleric from the first benefice, providing, of course, that the cleric does not attempt to hold the first benefice also, in which case trouble is unavoidable.

The canon under consideration[76] demands that before the cleric takes possession he must make the profession of faith when it is a question of those benefices

74. Santi, *op. cit.*, Vol. III, No. 31, Tit. VII.
75. Canon 188, 3.
76. Canon 1443.

requiring such profession. Benefices which require the profession are, according to canon 1406, 1. 7, all benefices, even manual, which have the care of souls; and paragraph 2 demands that when a cleric acquires a new benefice, after giving up his former, he must again make the profession. The profession must be made according to the formula approved by the Holy See and found in the copies of the Code.[77] Trent prescribed this profession to be made within two months after taking pos-ses-sion of the benefice. The Code changes this law by insisting that it be taken before the cleric is installed. The neglect to make his profession has serious consequences, as can be seen from canon 2403, which says that, if a cleric has neglected to make it without being excused by a just impediment, he is to be warned and given a certain time to make it; after which time he is considered contumacious and is to be punished by privation of his benefice; moreover he does not make the revenue of the benefice his own in the meantime. The legitimate time, then, to make it, is before taking possession, and if it is then neglected, the bishop should warn the cleric and give him a certain time to comply with the rules, after which time he is to be deprived of his benefice. The loss of revenue by one who has failed to make it needs no declaratory sentence, according to the more common opinion of canonists. Nor does ignorance nor a contrary custom excuse from this punishment. Canon 1408 tells us that any contrary custom is to be reprobated, and canon 27 says that any custom which is reprobated expressly in the law is not reasonable and therefore can never acquire the force of law or prevent the action of any law.

The profession must be made before the bishop or his delegate and must be made personally. A procurator may not be substituted for this purpose. Even before

77. Sess. XXIV, c. 12, de Ref.

the Code it was the common teaching of canonists that this profession is to be made personally, although there were not lacking great authors, such as Sanchez, Barbosa, Reiffenstuel, Schmalzgrueber and others who held that it could be made through a procurator. The reason for this is evident; it is the purpose of the Church to provide in all ways possible that her ministers be proved faithful to her teaching and to see that no one is sent to teach others who himself has not the faith. It is merely a precautionary measure but had its origin in the history of men losing the faith, although teaching it to others.

Besides the profession of faith, the cleric, before taking possession of his benefice, must also take the oath against modernism. From canon 6, 6, it would appear that this oath is no longer binding. It is not mentioned in the Code and the cited canon says that any laws not mentioned in the Code are considered to have lost their binding force. In virtue, however, of a decree of the Sacred Congregation of the Holy Office, 22 March, 1918, the regulations regarding this oath will still continue in force, even after the Code, until the Holy See ordains otherwise. The prescriptions against modernism, made on account of the errors which are creeping in at the present, are of their nature, temporary and transitory, and therefore could not be incorporated into the Code, which gives only permanent laws. Until, however, the poison of modernism has spent its force, the need for all precautions will be admitted, and consequently a cleric obtaining a parochial benefice must give this proof of his stand against the error.

CHAPTER VII

Rights and Obligations of Beneficiaries

1. *Spiritual and Temporal Rights*

After legitimately taking possession of a benefice a cleric enjoys all the rights, both spiritual and temporal, which are attached to the benefice. We have already noticed in passing, that this is one of the effects of canonical installation. The rights of a beneficiary are, then, both spiritual and temporal. The spiritual rights arise from the sacred office, which is an integral part of every benefice. They will differ according as the offices differ. The rights of the bishoprics are entirely different from those attached to the office of a parochial benefice. It is not our purpose here to go into detail concerning the spiritual rights connected with benefices as they are too varied to be treated within such narrow limits. The rights of a cleric holding a parochial benefice can be determined from those parts of the Code treating of parishes and pastors. The temporal rights of a benefice arise from the revenue connected with the benefice. It is the consideration of these temporal rights which differentiates the concept of a benefice from that of a parish. We have seen in numerous places that the subject—parochial benefices—is treated from one angle or another in different parts of the Code. In the second book those aspects connected with spiritual rights are treated, while the question of revenue is reserved to that part of the third book under consideration. We shall, therefore, try to discover what laws regard the temporal revenues of benefices and what rights the beneficiary has over this temporal revenue.

2. *Sources of Revenue*

The revenue of a cleric may be divided into *beneficial, patrimonial* and *quasi-patrimonial.* The fruits of the benefice constitute the beneficial revenue, while inheritances received from external sources make up the patrimonial revenue. Whatever a cleric acquires from spiritual work, other than that of his benefice, is called quasi-patrimonial, an example of which would be that received for preaching in a neighboring church. In the old law stole fees were also considered quasi-patrimonial revenue, but the definition of benefice revenue given in canon 1410 includes, as we have seen, stole fees under the title of beneficial revenue wherever the stole fees are made part of the revenue of the beneficiary. In the United States stole fees are usually considered quasi-patrimonial, as they are something over and above the salary of the pastor. If, however, the bishop, in erecting a parish, determines that the stole fees will constitute part of the official revenue of the parish, they will become beneficial revenue, subject to the laws which we are about to consider.

3. *Disposition of the Revenue of a Benefice*

It has been the constant teaching of the Church that a cleric does not lose his capability of receiving patrimonial or quasi-patrimonial money nor his ability to freely dispose of it in whatsoever way he desires. In this he is like other people and can dispose of it either while living, or after death by will. But such is not the case with beneficial revenue. Canon 1473 says that the beneficiary can freely use benefice money for his decent support, even though he have other money not belonging to the benefice; but whatever is over and above what is necessary for his support must be spent in helping the poor or for other worthy causes. The words "decent support" do not mean merely food, clothes and lodging, but also whatever is necessary for moderate hospitality and recreation, and something for his books and other quasi-essentials. It is intended that he be able to live up to his station in life without luxury.

Trent[78] treats this question very severely and tells bishops and others that those undertaking the offices of the Church should remember that they are called, not to a life of luxury, but of work, and that they should give the example, by their lives, of frugality and modesty which will commend them to the faithful. "Wherefore, following in the footsteps of the Council of Carthage, this synod orders bishops not only to be satisfied with modest furniture and table, and with frugal food, but warns them that nothing appear in the rest of their life or home which is foreign to this sacred institute, or whatever does not show simplicity, zeal for souls and contempt for vanities. It wholly forbids them to increase the goods of their relatives or family with the revenue of the church, since also the canons of the Apostles forbid that ecclesiastical goods, which belong to God, be given to relatives; but if the relatives be paupers, let them be given as paupers; but let not the bishop take away or dissipate the goods for them; indeed, as far as possible, this synod warns them to put away any human affection toward brothers, nephews and relatives, as it is the root of many of the evils of the Church. And what has been said of bishops, is to be observed by all those having ecclesiastical benefices, both secular and regular, according to the condition of their rank."[79] This passage gives the keynote to the whole question of ecclesiastical revenue and from it we can gather the idea of the Church in placing revenue into the hands of clerics. He is to use it insofar as it is necessary for his support, so that he may carry on his spiritual work, but he may not go beyond that.

The question of whether or not the cleric holding a

78. Sess. XXV, c. 1, de Ref.
79. Trent, *loc. cit.*

benefice acquires ownership to this revenue has long been disputed. Those who hold the negative allege, for their opinion, the words of the Fathers of the Church, who call the goods of the Church the *vota* of the faithful, the price of sins, and the patrimony of the poor; from which they deduce that the clerics do not acquire ownership of these goods, but only the use of them insofar as it is necessary, and that those doing otherwise are called robbers, thieves, oppressors of the needy, murderers of the poor, etc. Secondly, they refer to the times when all church goods were had in common and administered by the bishops insofar as each cleric needed them and no more. After this common life was discontinued, they say, the nature of these goods did not change, nor did the clerics obtain any title over the superfluous goods. But the more common opinion of canonists is that they do acquire ownership over not only the necessary portion, but also over the rest of the revenue. In proof of their opinion they allege the words of Trent, saying that clerics not observing the law of residence do not make the revenue their own (*non facit fructus suos*); and by induction they claim that those who do observe this law of residence do make the revenue their own.

Therefore, following the opinion more commonly held today, we may hold that clerics do obtain ownership over all the revenue, but not that they may dispose of them as they wish. A person may have the ownership of a thing without having the free disposal of it, and consequently a beneficiary must be said to have the ownership but with the obligation of distributing the superfluous among the poor or some other worthy cause. Whether this obligation be one of justice or charity, or merely ecclesiastical precept, is also disputed; but with De Angelis and others we think that it is merely from ecclesiastical precept. One of the recent commentators on the Code[80] agrees that it is not

80. Creusen-Vermeersch, *Summa Novi Juris Canonici*, 1919, No 567.

from justice but from the virtue of religion. The Code, by omitting any mention of an obligation of justice, seems to lend weight to this opinion against the opinion that it is of justice. And according to canon 239 cardinals have the power to dispose of this revenue by will, which would not be possible if there were an obligation in justice of spending the superfluous for the poor. Therefore, if a cleric would dispose of the superfluous goods otherwise than for the poor, he would indeed be guilty of grave sin, but the obligation of restitution could not be imposed on him because of the probability of the above opinion.

4. *Beneficial Revenue in the United States*

In the United States the revenue received by the pastor is determined in various ways, according to the customs of different localities. In some places the pastor receives a salary and, in addition, the expenses of the house are borne by the parish. The living expenses are taken directly from the parish fund and the salary is considered as the amount necessary for his support over and above his rectory expenses. In this supposition the salary is received in fee simple and whatever he saves from it is considered parsimonial revenue and belongs to him. Any money he saves in household expenses by living frugally belongs not to him, but to the parish. In other places the salary received by the pastor covers household expenses, and in this supposition whatever the pastor saves by living sparingly belongs to him as parsimonial revenue. In some dioceses it is customary to give the Easter and Christmas offerings to the pastor. We have noticed that although stole fees may be considered part of the revenue, still in this country they are not included, and hence the pastor, in determining the amount of his revenue, need not consider them.

The revenue, therefore, of the parish, consists of

the offerings of the faithful, and the amount of it received by the pastor is the salary plus his living expenses, or in some cases, the salary, which includes living expenses. The remainder of the church money is to be expended for the poor or other worthy causes, according to the common law as found in canon 1473. But on account of the prevailing conditions, the remainder of the money is used up in church expenses and for the upkeep of the school, etc., so that instead of a surplus there is usually scarcely enough for everything. It is very doubtful whether there are any dioceses in this country where all the money which comes into the parish is at the disposal of the pastor, as in some Catholic countries where the idea of benefices has been followed more closely than here.

5. *Beneficiaries Attached to Religious Institutions*

A religious pastor is subject to some special rules with regard to the ownership, investment and handling of money. His vow of poverty necessitates some regulations in this regard and we find them established in the Code in the second book under the heading *"De religiosis."* It is a general principle that whatever a religious priest acquires is acquired for the order to which he belongs. In the case of a religious pastor it is not always easy to apply the rule because a parishioner may give him money with the intention that it be applied to the parish and not mention explicitly its purpose. The Code, then, says that goods which come to him *"intuitu paroeciae,"* over which he rules, are acquired for the parish; all other goods are acquired for his religious brethren.[81] If, then, a person gives him money as a pastor, it belongs to the parish; but if the money is given him in a personal way, it belongs to the Order.

Again, the vow of poverty forbids all acts of owner-

81. Canon 630, 3.

ship independent of the consent of the Superior. But a pastor is frequently obliged to exercise acts of ownership, and if he were obliged to ask permission in each case it would be morally impossible for him to hold a parish. Canon 630, 4, gives a working rule which is very practical, and facilitates such acts. The canon cited says that he can in any lawful way accept alms or even collect them, for the good of his parishioners, or for the parish school, or for other worthy causes connected with the parish, and can administer this money and give it to particular persons or to the school or worthy cause, in keeping with the intention of the givers, according to his own prudent judgment, without the knowledge or consent of the Superior. The only power that the Superior has in this matter is to keep a vigilant watch over him so that he will not overstep the bounds marked out by the canon. In allowing one of his subjects to be a pastor the Superior is considered as giving this permission.

The religious pastor is not so free with regard to money for building, conserving, restoring or decorating his church. In order to accept, retain, collect or administer money for these purposes, he requires the consent of his superior if the parish belongs to the Order; otherwise he requires the consent of the Ordinary. This is a most just and reasonable rule because if the church belongs to the religious order it is right that the religious Superior should have the power to decide questions of building, renovating, decorating, etc., and if such church belongs to the Ordinary, the religious pastor should be subject to him in this regard, as are all the other priests of the diocese. The regulations of this last paragraph regarding the permission of the Superior are entirely new, and, according to a recent commentator, seem impractical.[82] This canonist thinks

---

82. Augustine, *A Commentary on Canon Law*, Vol. 111, page 361.

that the Order will need a host of officials to keep the records of the parishes under its control if such numerous details must be referred to the Superior in every case. But the intent of the law seems to be to give the Superior control over certain dealings of the parish so that if he wishes to prevent the action of the pastor he need only withhold his consent.

Whenever it is necessary or advisable to invest the funds of the parish, the religious pastor is bound to obtain the permission of the Ordinary before acting.[83] This applies to all moneys given to the parish or mission, or money given to the religious himself for a parochial or missionary purpose. Money given to church or mission is either: pew rent, receipts from seats, church collections, collections taken up at lectures in favor of the church, house collections or subscriptions. To invest (*pro collatione pecuniae*) is to spend money in the purchase of property, for instance, government or other bonds, shares in stock companies, etc. But it is not investing money to put it into a bank, even though put there with the intention of obtaining interest; for money is put into banks in order to facilitate trading by checks and drafts. Therefore, the consent of the Ordinary is not necessary for banking money. The text of the canon states that any money (*cujusvis pecuniae*), little or great, must not be invested without the consent of the Ordinary.

6. *The Obligation of Receiving Orders*

Under this title of rights and obligations of beneficiaries, the Code says, in canon 1474, that whenever the reception of any Order is required in order to obtain a benefice, the beneficiary should receive the order before being appointed to the benefice. This canon should really be found among the rules for appointment to benefices,

83. Canon 533, 4.

because it is neither a right nor a duty of a *beneficiary* to receive such Order, because it is something which precedes his being a beneficiary. A man is not a beneficiary until he has received the Order and is appointed to the benefice. However, it is the traditional place to mention this rule and with some reason, because prior to the Code a man could be appointed to a parochial benefice who was not in Sacerdotal Orders and he then had the obligation of receiving the required Order within a year.

We see from canon 188 that only clerics can obtain benefices. This is the old law on the subject, and from it we gather the general principle that a person must be tonsured at least before obtaining any benefice. Benefices which have the care of souls, either in the external or internal forum, cannot be validly given to one who is not a priest.[84] Hence the practice formerly sanctioned by custom of conferring a parochial benefice on a cleric who was not a priest, but with the obligation of receiving the priesthood within a year, is now justifiable no longer. There is no Order demanded by the law for simple benefices, and hence we must consult the customs of the Church or the provisions of the founders. When no certain Order is demanded by these, tonsure is sufficient.

7. *The Obligation of Personal Service*

A person obtaining a benefice is obliged to perform, with diligence and fidelity, the office attached to the benefice. This duty arises from the very nature of a benefice, for benefices are given on account of an office, as we have seen above. Moreover, the beneficiary is bound to perform this office personally because whatever is done by a substitute is usually done with less care than if the beneficiary performed it. Again, the benefice

---

84. Canon 154; 453, 1.

is erected to support one person, not two; and there is made provision for one only in the matter of revenue. The principle that whatever is done personally may also be done through a procurator does not apply to beneficiaries because a beneficiary is selected by reason of his qualities, and hence he cannot give over the office to another. The principle should be understood with this restriction: unless some grave cause permits the beneficiary to assign a substitute, or where it is necessary to have assistants in order to properly attend to all the wants of the benefice. When the benefice is too large for the one person to take care of it, as in the case of large parishes, the pastor may have assistants to help him in the work, but he may not on that account give up the care of it to them. They are merely helpers and he has the first obligation in performing the duties of the benefice.

8. *The Recitation of the Divine Office*

There is imposed on the person of the beneficiary the obligation of reciting the divine office. Usually the beneficiary is in major Orders and already has the obligation of the office, but it can happen that the cleric not in Major Orders obtains a simple benefice, and will be obliged by reason of his office to the recitation of the breviary. If the beneficiary does not satisfy the obligation of the canonical hours without being excused by a just reason, he does not obtain the fruit of the benefice in proportion to the time during which he has omitted it; it must then be given to the building fund of the church, or to the diocesan seminary, or to some other worthy cause.[85] This is a repetition of the old law on the subject. But the opinion of recognized authors is that there will very often be a reasonable excuse for not making restitution because many of the Doctors con-

85. Canon 1475.

sidered that in curata benefices (and St. Alphonsus thought it probable) the greater part of the revenue is assigned as a *compensation* for the other offices which the beneficiary has charge. Therefore, a pastor who administers the sacraments, teaches the catechism, and does other work, should not be deprived of all his revenue because he omitted the recitation of the office.[86] This opinion can readily be applied to the pastors in this country because the care of souls demands constant labor on the part of the pastor, even more so than in most Catholic countries.

St. Pius V gave the following rule for those omitting the recitation of the breviary: those who omit the entire office lose the whole fruit for the day; those who omit matins, lose one-half of the fruit corresponding to the day; those who omit the rest of the office also lose one-half, while those who omit a small hour lose one-sixth of the revenue of the day. The only benefices in which the above rule can be applied to are those which have only the duty of reciting the office.

9. *The Beneficiary as Administrator*

The beneficiary also has the obligation of administrating the goods of the benefice because he is the guardian. If he is culpably negligent in the administration and the benefice suffers a loss, he is bound to repair the damage, and the Ordinary is obliged to make him make up the loss, and if he be pastor, the Ordinary may remove him from his office. The ordinary expenses of administration and of collecting the revenues of the benefice must be paid by the beneficiary; while extraordinary expenses incurred in repairing the residence of the beneficiary must be paid by those who are obliged to make these repairs, unless the charter of foundation or legitimate agreements or customs provide otherwise.

---

86. Genicot, *Institutiones Theologiae Moralis*, Vol. II, Art. 47, part 3, 1905.

Minor repairs which the beneficiary must make at his own expense, should be made as soon as possible in order to avoid greater damage. Such is the common law with regard to repairs and administration of beneficial goods and property. In this country the pastor is never compelled to make any repairs with the money given him as salary.

The law will apply only to those places where all the money coming into the parish fund is at the disposal of the pastor as benefice revenue. In the United States the amount of money paid in the pastor's salary is simply enough for his decent support, and the remainder is put into the church treasury. When repairs are necessary the church fund must bear the expenses, or the pastor must appeal to the people for the required money. The only obligation the pastors in this country will have, therefore, from these canons, will be to watch over the church property and take steps to have repairing done when it becomes necessary. If he fails to take the necessary interest in the upkeep of the property, he may be removed from his parish as the canon directs. The Ordinary is instructed to ascertain whether or not the pastor is doing his duty in this regard, and in ascertaining this he may use the rural deans as his agents. The obligation, however, rests with the Ordinary, and devolves upon the rural deans only when appointed to that work by the Ordinary.

When church money or property is loaned or leased, the beneficiary may not collect the interest money for more than six months in advance without the consent of the Ordinary, and when this permission is given, the Ordinary will provide, by appropriate precautions, that such collection does not result in damage, either to the successor or to a pious institution. In other words, the beneficiary may not collect the revenue of the benefice more than six months in advance without the express consent of the Ordinary. If the beneficiary dies or is removed from office in the meantime, there may be difficulty for the successor to receive the money; hence the precautions by the Ordinary. The annual revenue must be divided between the successor and the predecessor (or his heirs in case of death) in proportion to the time either has served the benefice, taking into account all the revenues and expenses, unless legitimate custom or particular statute provide otherwise. Therefore, if the predecessor was in office for half the year, he or his heirs receive half the revenue, less current expenses.[87]

10. *Administration of a Benefice During a Vacancy*

When a benefice is vacant a substitute is appointed to take charge as the vicar and he is given a suitable salary. The remainder of the funds of the benefice goes to the endowment fund and the building fund in equal parts, except where legitimate custom provides that all the fruit goes to the diocese.[88] Custom here provides that the vicar receives a suitable salary and the remainder of the funds of the parish go to the parish fund as usual.

11. *Administration of Episcopal Funds*

The episcopal funds should be carefully administered by the bishop. His residence should be kept in good condition, and if repairs are required, the expenses must be paid from the funds of the bishop unless others are obliged by particular reasons to defray these expenses. The bishop shall also see to it that an accurate inventory is made of all the furniture and movable goods belonging to the episcopal residence, and provide that they shall be transmitted in their entirety to his successor.[89]

---

87. Canon 1476-1480.
88. Canon 1481.
89. Canon 1483.

CHAPTER VIII

The Loss of Ecclesiastical Benefices

1. *The Various Ways of Losing a Benefice*

Although all benefices, with the exception of religious benefices, are by common law subjectively perpetual, nevertheless there are ways and reasons for which they may become vacant. Under the title of benefices the Code mentions only two ways, namely, by resignation and by exchange of benefices. But in looking over the Code we find, for instance, that in the second book are given some general rules for the loss of ecclesiastical offices, under which title benefices are included. Again, in the fourth book are given the rules for administrative removal and transfer of a particular kind of beneficiary, the parochial beneficiary. In this chapter, therefore, we will treat of the ordinary ways by which a benefice may become vacant.

2. *Resignation of a Benefice*

Resignation of a benefice may be defined as the voluntary giving up of one's benefice for a just cause, before a legitimate authority who accepts it. Before the distinction was made between the conferring of Orders and the assigning to a benefice, resignations were rare. But after this distinction was admitted, it became legitimate to resign a benefice, when done in accord with the law.

Resignation of a benefice is either express or tacit. Express resignation is that act by which the desire of giving up of a benefice is declared either in writing or orally, according to the form prescribed by the law.

Tacit resignation is that procedure by which the giving up of a benefice is made known not in words but by the interpretation of the law.

Canon 184 tells us that every cleric who is in his right mind can, for a just cause, resign his ecclesiastical office unless prohibited by some special law. The authors in discussing the causes say that *necessity* or *great utility to the Church* are just causes. Innocent III[90] gave a list of causes which can be summed up in the versicle: *"debilis, ignarus, male consciens, irregularis; quem mala plebs odit, dans scandala, cedere possit."* Weakness from old age or infirmity; lack of knowledge (in which case resignation is not forced but advised); those crimes which even after penance are obstacles to performing his duties; irregularity which prevents the beneficiary from doing his work; hatred of the people, even when he is innocent, and those who have given such scandal that their usefulness is impaired. These causes are the usual ones for resignation but not the only causes which may allow a cleric to resign. The cause must be just and the justice can be determined from the utility or necessity of the Church. Canon 189 instructs Superiors not to accept resignations without a just and proportionate cause.

The resignation of a benefice should be accepted by the legitimate Superior; for, just as a cleric cannot of his own authority take possession of a benefice, so also he cannot of his own authority leave it. The Superior must either accept or reject it within the time stated in the law; canon 189 says that for those offices within the province of the Ordinary, he must either accept or reject resignations within a month. With the acceptance, the benefice becomes vacant and not before. The beneficiary then loses all right to the benefice, and if he again wishes to obtain it he must go through the formality of

---

90. Cap. 10, Tit. IX, Lib. I.

being appointed and installed, as he has not the privilege of recalling his resignation.[91]

Those offices are vacant by *tacit* resignation which are mentioned in canon 188, namely:

1. If the beneficiary makes a religious profession. In this case parochial benefices are vacant one year after the profession; other benefices are vacant after three years.[92] All religious professions are included under this rule.[93]

2. If the beneficiary neglects to take possession within the time prescribed by law; or where the law prescribes no definite time, within the time prescribed by the Ordinary. The time prescribed, for instance, for bishops taking possession of their dioceses, is four months.[94] Canon 1444, 2, instructs Ordinaries to determine the time within which the newly appointed beneficiary will take possession. This time is "*tempus utile*" as expressed in the canon under consideration, and hence does not lapse if the beneficiary is prevented from taking possession.[95] Needless to say, the Ordinary should make the time as short as possible unless circumstances move him to make the time longer than usually needed.

3. If the beneficiary accepts and retains possession of incompatible benefices, as we have already seen. In this case both benefices become vacant.

4. If the beneficiary publicly renounces the faith. This does not include mere schism if unconnected with heresy, although the Ordinary may by process of law remove one guilty of schism, but not on the strength of this canon. The offence is public, according to canon 2197, 1, either if it is already public or in such circumstances that one can prudently judge that it can become public easily.

---

91. Canon 191.
92. Canon 584.
93. Canon 584.
94. Canon 333.
95. Canon 35.

5. If the beneficiary contracts what is called a civil marriage.

6. If the beneficiary joins the army of his own accord contrary to the prescription of canon 141, 1, which allows the Ordinary to give the required permission in cases where he joins voluntarily in order to free himself the sooner from the service. This may happen in countries where military service is compulsory.

7. If the beneficiary puts off the ecclesiastical habit without just cause and does not again resume it within a month after being warned by the Ordinary.

8. If the beneficiary fails to observe the law of residence, and after warning from the Ordinary does not obey within the time specified by the Ordinary, unless prevented by a just impediment.

So far we have been considering unconditional resignation or that resignation made without any agreement attached to it. Conditional resignation is that form of resignation which is made under some condition, agreement, or when a condition or agreement is added in favor of the person resigning, or of a third party. Conditional resignations are, as a rule, forbidden by the law, but when some necessity arises for receiving them they are allowable. The usual person, however, to receive a conditional agreement is the Pope; the power of the bishop being greatly restricted. Canon 1486 gives the faculty of the Ordinary in receiving these conditional agreements, namely: The Ordinary cannot accept a resignation made in favor of another, nor one made under a condition which affects the appointment to the benefice or its revenues; the only exception being that he may accept the resignation of one of the parties of a dispute when made in favor of the other party to the dispute. The danger of conditional resignations is that of hereditary succession, as a cleric may resign on his deathbed and name a relative to succeed him, which would be against the very spirit of the laws. It would, in the first place, greatly diminish the power of the Ordinary in making appointments, and would originate a custom that a certain benefice belongs to a certain family to the exclusion of all other clerics. Another form of conditional resignation concerns the revenue, when, for instance, a cleric resigns with the agreement that he receive a pension. We have seen above when a pension may be given a cleric from a benefice, but a resignation made with that agreement would not be valid, according to the canon under consideration.

There are two exceptions to the general laws on resignations with regard to resignations of benefices. Canon 1484 forbids Ordinaries to accept the resignation of a cleric in Major Orders unless it is certain that he has sufficient funds to support him; and when it is a question of a man entering a religious order, the resignation does not take place until after one year or three years, depending on whether the cleric had a parochial benefice or another form of benefice. The reason for the canon is plain; it is the wish of the Church that all Her ministers be provided for in a becoming way. It is not becoming for a cleric to engage in occupations which do not befit his state in life, and therefore She has established the benefices to insure him support. When, then, a man desires to leave his benefice and its support, it is necessary that he have a fitting way to live. It does not seem against the spirit of this canon to accept a pastor's resignation and make him an assistant in some parish. This would provide him with support in a becoming way as demanded by the canon. Or he may resign if he has enough patrimonial or quasi-patrimonial revenue to provide him for life. The judgment as to what is necessary in this case is left to the Ordinary in every case, as the law speaks directly to Ordinaries. If the cleric disagrees with the opinion of the Ordinary in this matter, he has the privliege of recourse to a higher authority to settle the disagreement.

The second exception to the general rule on resignations which the Code makes for benefices is in canon 1485, which says that the resignation of a benefice to the title of which the cleric was ordained, is null unless express mention is made in the resignation of that fact, and another title substituted with the consent of the Ordinary. According to canons 979 and 981, the legitimate titles for ordination are, besides that of benefice, the titles of patrimony, pension and service of the Church, and for places subject to the Congregation of the Propaganda, also the title of mission service. If, then, a cleric resigns his title of benefice, he must supply himself with another of the above titles with the consent of the Ordinary.

3. *Exchange of Benefices*

In the second place a benefice can be lost by exchange, which is the reciprocal resignation of two benefices with the intention that each cleric obtain the benefice of the Order. In order to effect this exchange it is sufficient that both have the title to their benefices, that both make their resignation into the hands of the superior authority, and that after resignation each obtains the benefice of the other. The resignations may be tendered in person, or in writing, or even through a procurator having a special mandate for that purpose. Canon 1487 tells us that the exchange of two benefices cannot be validly executed by the Ordinary unless on account of the necessity of the Church, or utility to the Church or for some other just cause, made without injury to others, and with the consent of the Ordinary. The just cause is necessary, then, for validity, but to the usual causes, utility and necessity of the Church, the Code adds the permission to act on any other just cause. Prior to the Code the authors considered utility and necessity of the Church as the only justifying causes and said that the utility and necessity of the clerics did not suffice unless they also affected the Church. Now any just cause will be sufficient and the Ordinary is, in this, as in resignations, the competent judge. Examples of just causes would be, for instance, where the climate does not agree with the health of one or both of the beneficiaries, or when one of the clerics has incurred the hatred of the people, or if one man could do better work in the second benefice than the present beneficiary.

The Ordinary is obliged to either accept or reject the proposed exchange within a month and the exchange goes into effect from the moment he agrees to it. The consent of the Ordinary in making exchanges is in agreement with the law on taking possession, which we have considered above. For no cleric can take possession of a benefice of his own authority.

The Ordinary is the only official in the diocese capable of accepting the resignation made with the idea of exchange. The vicar-general is expressly excluded unless he has a special mandate for the purpose; and the vicar of the chapter (or administrator, in this country) is also excluded. Exchange really amounts to conferring a new parish on a cleric and as the Ordinary is the only authority to confer parishes, so also in exchance he is the only person competent to do it. It preserves to him the ruling of his diocese without any interference from the vicar general except in such cases as he delegates the vicar general. As for the vicar of the chapter during the vacancy of the diocese, he has less power in this matter than in the actual conferring of parishes, because, as we have seen, he may confer parishes when the See has been vacant for a year; but there is no such exception made for him in the matter of exchange of benefices.

As the power of the vicar-general and vicar of the chapter are limited, so also the power of the Ordinary is limited with regard to the kind of benefices he may exchange. He may not exchange beneficiaries of parishes which are reserved to the Holy See, whether both or only one of them be reserved. This is not a new limitation, as we have seen that his power over reserved benefices is limited with regard to appointment as well as any other canonical change. It would seem, also, that the power of Ordinaries is limited with regard to exchanges in benefices united with monasteries or other moral persons, and also with regard to benefices united to other benefices, even though the effects of the union have not yet been put into execution. For canon 1487, in giving ordinaries to make this exchange, allows it only when others do not suffer injury. But if the Ordinary were to make exchanges in these benefices he would surely inflict injury on the rights of the monasteries or others to which the benefices are united. The authors prior to the Code, commenting on exchange, held that the Ordinary had no faculty in these cases, and although the Code itself does not mention them explicitly, nevertheless from the words, "*sine aliorum detrimento,*" we can conclude that his power is still limited. The authors also held that benefices which were in dispute could not be exchanged because while there is a dispute about the title, nobody can be said to possess it. And one of the essentials in this matter of exchange is that the parties have the title to their benefices.

If the benefices to be exchanged are unequal either in revenue or honor, no compensation may be made by reservation of fruits or by payment of money or any other thing valuable at a price. This would be simony of the divine and natural law, and the exchange would be invalid. Nor is the Ordinary permitted to put into execution what is called a triangular exchange, that, namely, where three benefices are involved, A obtains B's benefice, while B obtains C's benefice, and C obtains A's benefice. For while in substance this is merely a double exchange, nevertheless too many agreements about exchange are considered dangerous. Therefore, nobody but the Holy Father can effect a change between more than two persons.

4. *The Transfer of Beneficiaries*

The third manner of losing a benefice is by transfer which may be defined as the change of a person from one benefice to another made for a reason by superior authority. In the early days transfers were seldom made, but in recent times they became more frequent, possibly on account of the changing circumstances of the times. The old doctrine on the subject was that a cleric could not be transferred against his will, although it was discussed even from the time of the Decretals, whether or not a man could not be transferred even against his will, provided he obtained a benefice as good or better than the one he formerly held. Some authors held that it could not be done, but when a cleric was unwilling, he could be removed from his benefice, providing, of course, that there was some good reason for the transfer. They said that he could be removed from the benefice on account of disobedience and that he was not given another benefice because of the law that a man could not be given a benefice unwillingly. Others held that such a beneficiary could be transferred even against his will when utility or necessity demanded it. Wernz[96] says that although a man could not generally be transferred against his will in the former centuries, nevertheless, *per modum exceptionis*, the bishop could force the beneficiary to resign and compel him to accept another benefice. He cites the words of Urban III,[97] who, after he has forbidden the exchange of prebends with an intervening agreement, added an exception: "If,

96. *Op. cit.*, Vol. II, No. 517, seqq.
97. C. 5, X, *de rerum permutatione*, III, 19.

however, the bishop has investigated the necessary cause, he can lawfully transfer persons from one place to another, so that while they are less useful in one place, they may be more useful in another." The commentators on the Decretals took from this and other passages the doctrine that the transfer is sometimes permissible, even agains the will of the beneficiary. Now, the Code ruling is very clear on the subject and we have the explicit doctrine that removable pastors may be moved against their will, provided certain procedures are gone through; while irremovable pastors may not be transferred against their will without the consent of the Holy See.[98] The innovation which the Code has brought about is that irremovable pastors are not transferable against their will. Prior to the Code *all pastors were transferable in the same way,* although there are some who think that by reason of the *Maxima Cura* the removable *ad nutum* pastors in France, while becoming stable as to removal, could be transferred without the usual causes of necessity or utility of the Church, provided there was some good reason, while other pastors could be transferred against their will only for the canonical reasons, necessity or utility to the Church.[99] But the general opinion was that all pastors were transferable in the same way and for the same canonical reasons. Now, however, pastors are distinguished into removable and irremovable and the distinction is very important in this matter of transfer because the irremovable species cannot be transferred against their will without the consent of the Holy See. The Code, herefore, gives irremovable pastors more stability in this regard than they have had for centuries.

The procedure for transferring removable pastors can be summed up as follows: if the good of souls demands that a pastor be transferred, from a parish

---

98. Canon 2163.
99. Wernz, *op. cit.,* Vol. 5, No. 908, note 17.

which he rules well, to another parish, the Ordinary will propose the transfer and ask him to consent to it for the love of God and of souls.[100] If the pastor refused he must give his reasons in writing,[101] which reasons the Ordinary will consider in conjunction with two parish priest consultors. The consultors will also give the Ordinary their opinion as to the quality of the two parishes under consideration, and the Ordinary will decide whether or not to proceed with his purpose. If he proceeds, he will again ask the pastor to consent, and if the pastor again refuses, the Ordinary will command him to go to the new parish, giving him a certain time within which to obey, and telling him that after that time his parish will be declared vacant. If the pastor does not obey within the time prescribed, his parish is declared vacant.

Thus is settled a question which has been unsolved for centuries and which has been the subject of discussion on every side. The idea prevailing before the Code that the only reason for transferring one against his will was either utility or necessity of the Church has now been changed for the broader term, "the good of souls," regardless of how souls will profit from the change. We now have the canonical reason for transfer and the canonical form for it, and from the consideration of both we see that the bishop is given greater latitude in providing for the wants of his diocese without, however, taking away all the liberty from his priests. The priest is protected against any injustice by the privilege of recourse to the Holy See, and during such recourse the bishop is forbidden to give the parish in any permanent way to another priest,[102] thus preventing complications if the Holy See decides to reverse the decision of the bishop. It is of the greatest importance that the bishop

---

100. Canon 2162.
101. 2164.
102. Canon 2146.

have this power of administrative transfer, on account of the changing conditions in the dioceses, and especially in the United States, and all who consider the subject will admit that the legislator has formulaed a law which will be of almost limitless possibilities for good. The "*salus animarum*" has always been the "*suprema lex,*" but the canonical procedure has been so complicated and uncertain that bishops were not always free to put the principle into practice as they would have wished.

So far we have been discussing the transfer of unwilling clerics. As to the transfer of clerics who are willing, canon 193 tells us that they may be transferred for any just cause, and as transfer is usually a promotion and something to be desired, the law concerning just cause can be interpreted broadly, not necessarily in the restricted sense of utility or necessity to the Church. It has never been the practice of the Church to forbid clerics to ascend higher, and therefore, when they are willing to be promoted to another benefice, the bishop may act on any just cause.

Canon 194 gives the rule that in transfer the first office is vacant when the cleric takes canonical possession of the second office unless the law or the Superior decrees otherwise. This is merely a repetition of that other canon which we have seen above, namely, that an office is vacant by tacit resignation when the cleric comes into possession of another office.[103]

5. *Removal from a Benefice*

The last manner of losing a benefice to be discussed here is that of removal which is closely akin to transfer, differing in this only that while in transfer a cleric passes from one office to another, in removal it is not necessary that the cleric be given another benefice or office. The removal here considered is the *administrative removal,*

---

103. Canon 188, 3.

not the *judiciary removal.* It is understood that for a crime a pastor may be removed from his office by the judge, but here we are considering not the fact of a crime, but removal induced by a cause which makes his ministry harmful, or at least, inefficient. The administrative removal of a pastor, therefore, may be defined as the privation of a parochial benefice made by the Ordinary according to law, but without strict judicial process, of a pastor whose ministry has been seriously impaired, either on account of some fault or crime for which privation is not given in punishment, or for other grave canonical causes occurring without any crime, and after removal the pastor is given some other duty or a pension for his support.

Administrative removal of pastors and other beneficiaries is not a new thing in the law. It had its foreshadowings in the Decretals. Innocent III[104] enumerates various reasons for which bishops could be removed, as, for instance, when the bishop has incurred the hatred of the people. And this reason could be applied also to inferior benefices on account of their resemblance to bishoprics. The commentators on the decretals saw in this and other passages the faculty of removing beneficiaries administratively in certain cases. But they urged it more than the texts they cited, and so after a time the matter became a common law. In recent times, and especially in the last century, cases were frequently discussed by the Sacred Congregation, which gave canonists the occasion to discuss more at length the different causes and the procedure for putting this administrative removal into effect. But the thing was far from crystallized, and the decisions of the bishops were often reversed by the Congregations.

The *Maxima Cura* in 1910 therefore filled a lacuna in the law with the canonical reasons and the canonical

---

104. C. 10, *X de renuntiatione,* 1, 9.

procedure which were to be used in these cases, and so took the matter out of the hands of those who would use this faculty in an arbitrary fashion. This decree, however, applied, according to the 30th canon, to those who held parishes as their *proper* rectors. The doubt then arose as to whether the so-called parishes in this country were affected by it, and the Consistorial Congregation[105] replied in the affirmative, as it had replied on the 28th of the preceding February concerning England. Things remained in this state for about four years, when the Congregation was again asked whether the removable pastors in this country were included in the decree, "*Maxima Cura.*" The reply came in 1915 that they were not included and that they could be removed *at nutum* by the bishop according to the law of Baltimore.[106] The result was that the irremovable pastors were included, and the removable pastors were not included in the decrees of the *Maxima Cura*. The Code has now incorporated the prescriptions of the *Maxima Cura* almost wholly in the fourth book, but on account of the change in the parochial status of the pastors in this country, not only the irremovable but the removable as well, are included in the provisions concerning administrative removal.

The purpose of the administrative removal was declared in the 1915 decision to be none other than to make it more easy to remove one having the care of souls when it was expedient that he be removed. In the ancient discipline a pastor could be removed only after great difficulty and the Church being mindful of the axiom that "*parochi ministerium sit in Ecclesias constitutum non in commodum ejus, cui committur, sed in eorum salutem, pro quibus confertur,*" has decided that

105. 13 March, 1911.
106. *Acta Apostolicae Sedis*, 28th June, 1915; III Plen. Council Baltimore, Tit. 11, Cap. 5, No. 32.

any easy process should be put into practice to remedy the defect of the old law.

In the canons concerning removal of pastors, the Code has distinguished between the removable and the irremovable species. In the *Maxima Cura* not a word was said about this distinction, as all pastors were considered irremovable with the same degree of stability. We have noticed that the Code, in canon 454, 2, declares that while all pastors are permanent, nevertheless some enjoy more stability than others; and now, in the consideration of the process of removal, the Code prescribes the different methods required for the two classes. It is merely a difference of the officials connected with the procedure; the reasons for both classes are the same.

In the definition of administrative removal we said that it was the privation of a pastor whose ministry has been impaired either on account of some fault or crime for which privation is not given in punishment, or for some other grave canonical causes occurring without any crime. Canon 2147 gives specifically the canonical reasons for the removal of irremovable pastors, and canon 2157 applies the same reasons for the removal of removable pastors. Canon 2147 says that an irremovable pastor may be moved from his parish for a reason which makes his ministry harmful, or at least inefficient, even though this be without fault on his part.

These reasons are particularly:

1. Incapability or permanent infirmity of either the mind, or body, which renders him incapable of doing his work, if, in the judgment of the Ordinary, the situation cannot be remedied with the help of vicars. Trent[107] ordered bishops to give coadjutors or temporary vicars to illiterate or unskilled pastors, *or to otherwise provide for them.* Thus we see the beginning of the present law of the Code.

---

107. Sess. XXI, C. 6, de. ref.

2. Hatred of the people, although it be unjust and not universal, provided it be such that it impedes the useful ministry of the pastor, and there is no hope that it will quickly pass away. In an above paragraph we have given this law as taken from the Decretals as the foreshadowing of the whole process of administrative removal. Innocent III applied it to bishops, but on account of the similarity of parishes to bishoprics, the canonists did not hesitate to apply it to parishes also.

3. The loss of his good reputation among upright and serious people, whether this is caused by his manner of living, or from some ancient crime which the law has wiped away by prescription, or from too much familiarity with relatives or those with whom he lives, unless their dismissal sufficiently provides for his reputation. In this section of the causes, we find mention of a crime which, when committed, would justify canonical trial to remove the pastor, but on account of prescription, he is freed from the consequences of it. The reason for including it here is that although he may be free from the possible punishment, nevertheless, the knowledge of the crime would make the people distrust and shun him and thereby impair his work among them.

4. A probable occult crime, imputable to the pastor, from which the Ordinary prudently foresees that great offence can arise to the faithful in the future. According to the *Maxima Cura* the occult crime had to be certain, not probable, but on account of the difficulty of ascertaining certitude on account of the few persons who knew about it, the Code has removed the necessity for certitude and now requires only the probability that an occult crime was committed by the pastor. This cause is somewhat similar to the cause considered under No. 3; the difference being that in this case the Ordinary is able to act before the pastor has already lost his reputation.

5. Bad administration of temporal goods of the church or benefice with great loss to the church or benefice, provided this cannot be remedied by taking away from the pastor the administration of temporal goods or in some other way; and the cause is valid for removal regardless of how fruitfully he carries on the spiritual work of the benefice. The Ordinary need not wait until the pastor has already inflicted loss on the benefice by his bad administration, but may act as soon as it becomes morally certain that such effect will follow.

As this list of the Code is not exhaustive but merely "*demonstrative modo,*" we can here add two other reasons given by the *Maxima Cura* but omitted by the Code:

6. Neglect of pastoral duties and persevering after one or two warnings, namely, in things of importance, such as the administration of the Sacraments, the care of the sick, preaching the Gospel, or in the observance of residence.

7. Disobedience to the precepts of the Ordinary in matters of importance, after one or two warnings, such as the avoiding too much familiarity with any person or family, or caring properly for the house of God, or concerning the collection of parish taxes and the like. It is to be noted that in these last two causes the bishop must give warning once or twice to the pastor and notify him that he will be removed if he does not amend. The disobedience to the Ordinary in matters of great importance includes many more things than those mentioned explicitly, and therefore any disobedience in a serious matter will constitute sufficient ground for the Ordinary to start proceedings against the pastor. As said above, these causes are applicable to both the removable and irremovable pastors alike.

As to the actual process of removing pastors, there is a difference between that used for removable and that used for irremovable pastors. The process used for removing irremovable pastors is the same as the process prescribed by the *Maxima Cura,* with the exception of minor details, and with the important exception that the Ordinary needs only the *advice* of the synodal examiners and parish priest consultors, where formerly he needed their consent and vote.

The procedure, then, for removing irremovable pastors, starts with the discussion of causes by the Ordinary and two synodal examiners, and the invitation to resign. In this discussion the Ordinary will go over the reasons with the examiners to consider their truth and seriousness. Then the Ordinary notifies the pastor either by letter or verbally that he should resign, and specifies the time within which the resignation must be tendered. In the *Maxima Cura* this definite time was set at ten days.[108] For validity the invitation to resign must contain the reasons alleged by the Ordinary and the arguments upon which these reasons rest. If the pastor neither resigns nor asks for a delay, nor offers reasons for not resigning, the Ordinary will first make certain that the invitation was received and that the pastor was not prevented by a just impediment from replying. Having established these things, the Ordinary will immediately remove him from the parish and need not provide for him by giving him another parish or pension, as we shall see later is prescribed for those who either resign or give their reasons for not resigning and are removed.

If, at the invitation of the Ordinary, the pastor resigns, the Ordinary will immediately declare the parish vacant on account of resignation. The pastor, however, in his letter of resignation, need not give as his reasons those alleged by the Ordinary, but may substitute for them other reasons which will be less embarrassing, as, for instance, that he is resigning in obedience to the wishes of the Ordinary.

---

108. Rule 10, No. 4.

If, instead of resigning, the pastor wishes to oppose the reasons given by the Ordinary, he may ask for a delay in order that he may prepare his defense, and the Ordinary can, if he thinks it prudent, grant him a certain time within which to present his case. In the *Maxima Cura* it was specified that in this case the Ordinary could, with the consent of the examiners, give him ten or twenty days to prepare his statement, but the Code leaves the determination of the time to the Ordinary, without the consent of the two synodal examiners. When the pastor gives his statement, the Ordinary will examine it with the help of the same two examiners, and approve or reject the reasons given by the pastor. Here, again, is a difference in detail, for the former law required the pastor to present his defense in writing, while the Code does not mention the manner of presentation. If the Ordinary rejects these reasons, he will signify his decision to the pastor in the form of a decree of removal. Against this decree of removal is given the right of recourse, not to a higher authority, but to the same Ordinary, but the pastor must present his recourse within ten days. After the recourse has been placed with the Ordinary, the pastor will, within ten days more, present his reasons and new proofs to show why the decree of removal should not be sustained. These reasons the Ordinary will consider in conjunction, not with the two synodal examiners, but with two parish priest consultors, and either reject or approve them. If rejected, the decree of removal is the result, and the Ordinary, with the aid of the advice of the two examiners or consultors, according to which set of officials helped to decide the removal, will consider the advisability of placing the pastor in another parish or office, or of giving him a pension, according as circumstances warrant. A pastor who resigns is to be favored more than one who was removed if other things are equal.

Thus, in a summary fashion, is given the procedure for removing an irremovable pastor, and throughout the whole action we have noticed that it is the intention of the legislator to make the removal as quick as possible and at the same time give the pastor sufficient time to defend himself to the best of his ability. The mention of ten days shows us that this administrative removal is not to be prolonged after the fashion of trials, but expedited in every possible way. The formalities of trials are almost wholly done away with and the mere necessities remain.

The removal of *removable* pastors is much like that described above, except that it is shorter and no recourse is allowed against the decree of removal. After the pastor has presented his defense *in writing* (as formerly required by the *Maxima Cura*) and the Ordinary, with the advice of his synodal examiners, thinks that it is not sufficient to warrant his remaining in the parish, he does not remove the pastor but again invites his resignation, threatening removal if he does not resign within a given time. After the time is expired, the pastor is given the decree of removal, and is to be provided for as mentioned above concerning irremovable pastors, by receiving another parish, or by a pension, as the circumstances warrant.

After the Ordinary has given the final decree of removal for either an irremovable or a removable pastor, the pastor must leave the parochial residence as soon as possible, except in the case of a sick man who cannot be conveniently transferred from the house, in which case the Ordinary will allow him the exclusive use of the house as long as this necessity lasts.[109]

There are many details given in the *Maxima Cura* which, although they do not oblige under the new law, nevertheless, are worthy of notice and should be put

---

109. Canons 2147-2161.

into practice by the Ordinary in putting into execution this administrative removal. The first of these is contained in canon 10, par. 3, which says that in the invitation to resign, occasioned by an occult crime, the Ordinary should use only general terms in a written invitation and withhold details until the pastor appears in person to hear them in the presence of one of the examiners. This is a very wise rule and should be followed in practice, even though it has no binding force in the Code. Another rule, found in canon 11, par. 1, the *Maxima Cura* orders that the names of those giving information to the Ordinary should be withheld from the pastor if they so desire; indeed, even when they have not expressed the wish, but from the revelation of the names the Ordinary can prudently foresee that they would be exposed to annoyance. In the second paragraph of this same canon we read that facts which cannot be made public without fear of great offence to the people, or without danger of quarrels and the life, should not be put to writing, nor even mentioned except in a guarded way so as to prevent any consequences. Again, in canon 18, is a prohibition to the pastor that he may not stir up the people or promote public subscriptions in his favor, or do anything else which might prevent the legitimate exercise of ecclesiastical jurisdiction; otherwise he may be punished according to the gravity of his fault. While this sanction is not mentioned explicitly in the canons relative to administrative removal, nevertheless, the Ordinary may punish such a cleric according to the general principles governing such actions. Canon 19 decrees that the votes of the examiners should be given secretly, and the reason is evident; this manner of voting gives the officials greater freedom of action, and although not prescribed by the new procedure, should be put into execution by the Ordinary to save embarrassment to officials in case they wish to disagree with him. There is no necessity for him to act according to their vote and so it is no restraint on him to give them this liberty. The Code says that in case of sickness the pastor can be allowed the exclusive use of the parochial residence until such time as he can be removed without injury; and the *Maxima Cura* adds that in the meantime the new rector of the parish will seek some other temporary home in the parish. Canon 465, in dealing with residence, says that the pastor is bound by obligation to reside in the parochial home near the church; but the Ordinary can permit him for a just cause to reside elsewhere, provided the home be not so far removed from the church that the performance of his duties will suffer. The sickness of the removed pastor would then be a just reason for allowing the new pastor to live somewhere else than the parochial residence.

CHAPTER IX

Parochial Benefices in the United States

The principal reason for writing at such great length here on the subject of benefices is because it is the intention of the writer to establish that the parishes in the United States are real benefices, and as such are subject to the laws governing benefices. Prior to the publication of the Code no such argument could be sustained, but as we have said in many places during the course of this discussion, the status of the parishes has been changed in this country, and now, instead of being merely missions, they are raised to the dignity of canonical parishes. Canon 216 has been a revolutionary canon with regard to this country, and probably has done more to change the discipline of the Church in the United States than any other single canon in the Code. The change has been threatened for a long time and does not come altogether unexpectedly.

The history of the Church in this country has been one of constant growth and approach to the condition of those countries which have been under the rule of the common law for centuries. In the beginning we find the French and Spanish settlements bringing from their native countries very definite ideas about Church discipline, but contrary to expectation, these did not last. The parishes and benefices which they erected have all vanished. Shea, in his history of the Church, quotes the First Council of Baltimore as mentioning the only known benefice in the United States as in New Orleans,[110] and quotes the synod of New Orleans of 1844

110. Vol. 111, page 414.

as stating that there were no benefices in that diocese.[111] The same author says that canonical parishes were erected in New Mexico in 1801.[112] Shea also speaks of the displeasure of certain parties in the both Californias over the establishment of canonical parishes in 1841.[113] Putzer, in his first edition of the Commentary on Apostolic Faculties,[114] tells us that the Provincial Council of San Francisco hints that there are, in the province of San Francisco, canonical parishes ruled over by missionary priests not having the status of pastors.[115]

The Church had its greatest growth in the colonies settled by peoples other than the Spanish and French, and whatever of common law practices the Spanish and French had introduced, were soon lost. As we have it today, the Church started from very crude beginnings, and under such circumstances that it was impossible to conform to the laws governing parishes and the like. When the first bishop of Baltimore appointed priests, he sent them out with a sort of general care of the people in a more or less indefinite territory. Lack of organization, scarcity of priests, fluctuating population and lack of funds, were among the reasons which compelled him to do the best he could under the circumstances, without adhering strictly to the ideal methods prescribed by the common law.

The Second Council of Baltimore,[116] about seventy-five years after Bishop Carroll had held his first Synod, made some progress in the way of legislation concerning parishes. In Tit. III, Chap. IV, No. 111, this Council says that since it is contrary to the laws and customs of the Church, and to the efficient care of souls, to have many priests in the one territory exercising the care

---

111. Vol. IV, page 269.
112. Vol. IV, p. 298.
113. Vol. IV, p. 352.
114. 1886.
115. *Op. cit.*, No. 130.
116. 1866.

of souls, independently of each other, and that since this practice begets confusion and discord, the bishops are instructed to place one pastor over each single place, and, if necessary, give him assistants to help him do the work. Before that time parishes were not distinctly marked out, and indeed, even after this Council, parishes were not everywhere distinctly marked out as to limits. For we see the Third Council of Baltimore,[117] twenty years later, prescribing that through all the provinces, and especially in the larger cities, where there are many parishes, districts be assigned *ad instar paroeciae,* with definite limits for each church. This was in obedience to the Council of Trent,[118] which had ordered this division into districts. The Council of Baltimore added that in taking the name of parishes and pastors, it was not the intention that they should be irremovable. It considered the time at hand when some parishes should have this quality and legislated that every tenth pastor should be made irremovable. This number could not be increased by the bishops for twenty years after the promulgation of the Council. Nor did the Council intend that either the removable or the irremovable rectors be canonical pastors, but hoped to approach this discipline little by little as circumstances would allow. There was, on the part of Rome, the intention that canonical parishes should be erected by this Council, but after hearing the Ordinaries, Rome decided that the missionary status could be tolerated. It is plainly evident from the consideration of this Council that the Church was making rapid strides toward the common law ideal.

The parishes, both removable and irremovable, remained in this state until the publication of the *Maxima Cura* in 1910. This decree abolished throughout the world the removable *ad nutum* parishes. This was not its primary intent; the principal purpose being just the

---

117. 1884.
118. Sess. XXIV, de Ref. c. 13.

opposite, namely, to make it more easy to *remove* canonical pastors without a long and complicated trial. But in its provisions it contained prescriptions which wiped away the removability at will idea of canonical parishes. Our parishes were not canonical, as admitted by all canonists, but a doubt was engendered as to whether the prescriptions of the decree applied to them. Canon 30 said that it applied to all who held a parish in any title, as its proper rector—whether they be called perpetual vicars or desservants, *or any other name*—and the Congregation of the Consistory was asked whether it applied to the United States. The Congregation answered[119] in the affirmative, as it had done the preceding month with regard to the parishes in England. The decree legislated for *parishes* and by including the missions of this country, gave the impression that the time was at hand for canonical parishes here. Things remained in *statu quo* for about four years, when the Congregation was again asked whether the removable parishes were included in the decree *Maxima Cura*. This time the answer came in the negative,[120] and said that removable pastors could be removed *ad nutum* by the bishop, but the bishop should keep in mind the admonition of Baltimore not to use his right unless for a grave cause and with consideration of merits.[121] From the consideration of the fact that the irremovable pastors were included under the prescriptions of the *Maxima Cura*, and that the *Maxima Cura* legislated for *parishes*, it is not to be wondered at that some considered that there was good ground for the opinion that irremovable pastors were canonical pastors.

It remained for the Code to definitely settle the question, and we find the answer in canon 216, which says that the territory of each diocese should be divided

119. 13 March, 1911.
120. 28th June, 1915.
121. 111 Coun. Balt. *loc. cit.*, No. 32.

into distinct territorial parts, each with its particular church and determined people, and a particular rector as pastor; and these parts of the dioceses are parishes. The Church in this country lived under the jurisdiction of the Congregation of the Propaganda until 1908 as a missionary country, and as such was not bound by the common law of the Universal Church. Therefore, the law previous to canon 216, namely, that of Trent, cited above, did not bind as to the parts of a diocese being parishes. But in 1908 we were removed from the competence of the Propaganda and placed under the common law of the Church. Why did not the parishes then become canonical? And why did they not become canonical when the *Maxima Cura* was interpreted as applying to them in 1911? In 1915 the second interpretation stated that the *removable* parishes were not canonical insofar as they were not subject to the decree, and the decree applied to *parishes.* It seems that an explicit declaration was necessary to exclude removable parishes, and even as it remained, our irremovable parishes were affected, showing that they were governed by the same procedure in removal as canonical parishes. Does the law of Baltimore still prevent our parishes from obtaining that canonical status which is demanded by the Code? At least one diocese of the country has already declared in a synod that its parishes are canonical,[122] and this indicates that they consider the Baltimore Law to be no longer binding.

But what does Rome think about the application of this canon to the United States? We get the answer from a declaration of the Sacred Consistorial Congregation, 1 August, 1919.[123] This Congregation, within whose competency come all questions affecting the organization of dioceses, received from dioceses which were subject, prior to the *"Sapienti Consilio"* of 1908,

---

122. Boston Sixth Synod, 7 April, 1919, Nos. 21 and 60.
123. *Apos. Sedis Acta.*, Vol. XI, page 346.

to the Propaganda, many doubts concerning the nature of the parishes or missions into which these same dioceses were divided. After hearing many Ordinaries of these places the Congregation decreed that:

1. From canon 216 of the Code, it is undoubted that the parts of the aforesaid dioceses, over which a particular rector has been assigned for the care of souls, should in the future be considered parishes, and ought to be called by that name (*uti paroecias in posterum haberi atque eo nomine appellari debere*).

2. To constitute parishes is required a decree of the Ordinary, by which decree is determined the territorial limits, the parochial residence, and the revenue both for the church and that for the support of the pastor; but it is not necessary that irremovability be assigned to the rector; indeed, if just causes are present, removability can be declared in the very erection according to canons 1411, 4; 454, 3, and 1438.

3. But if the small number, or a fluctuating population, or the absolute lack of suitable means of support do not justify the erection of these churches into parishes; they will remain as subsidiary churches or chaplaincies within the confines of some parish until they can acquire their own parochial standing.

From the first paragraph of this response it is clearly evident that the parishes of this country are considered by Rome to be canonical, and that at last they have attained the standing that they merit. There is no reason why the vast majority of parishes here cannot qualify equally as much as those of other countries. They have as much stability as to people and organization, and can no longer be considered in that state of uncertainty which prompted the bishops in times past to request Rome to allow their missionary status. The above response tells us very plainly that they will not be so considered. The United States is explicitly included in this response because it is one of the countries which were subject to the Propaganda prior to 1908. The only doubt as to their canonical position can arise from the second paragraph which requires a decree of erection by the bishop before a parish becomes canonical. But from the tenure of the whole response it is evident that the second paragraph must be considered separately from the first paragraph, and understood to apply to the erection of *new* parishes, not to those districts which are already marked out. Otherwise the two paragraphs contradict each other; for the first unequivocally says that the parishes in this country are parishes, and makes no mention of the decree of erection. It is presumed that the decree of erection is sufficiently given by the bishop having marked out the limits of the parishes. Canon 1418 directs that the erection of benefices (and implicitly, parishes) should be made by a legitimate instrument in which are defined the place, foundation fund, and rights and rights and duties. But written erection was not necessary for validity in the old law, and as the law of the Code is merely a repetition of the old law on the subject, we must interpret it in the same way, and say that implicit intervention of the bishop is sufficient as far as validity is concerned. So those who would deny canonical status on this ground, have no foundation for their argument.

So far in this chapter we have been considering, not the standing as benefices, but the standing as canonical parishes of our parishes in this country. It is necessary to do this because if our parishes are not canonically erected they cannot be benefices. The two ideas are practically inseparable, and are considered so by the Code, which gives certain phases of legislation for them under the title of parishes, and other phases under benefices. It is not impossible to conceive a parish which is not a benefice, but it surely is impossible to conceive a benefice with the care of souls which is not at the same time a canonical parish. Therefore, we have spent much time in the discussion of the parochial status before beginning to apply the laws of benefices to this country.

Granting that our parishes are canonical, let us look at the question of benefices. Three things are necessary for a benefice: first, the sacred office; secondly, the right to the revenues of the endowment, and lastly the erection. That our parishes have the sacred office is beyond doubt or question. They have the second condition if to the sacred office is attached the right to receive the revenue from the certain and voluntary offerings of the faithful, or stole fees, or both. For these are the usual and possible sources of parish revenue here. It is well to note that it is not necessary that this revenue be sufficient for the support of the rectors, as there is nothing in the definition[124] to that effect. Canon 1415 states that a benefice should not be erected unless with a sufficient endowment, but this does not imply that if the endowment is not suitable, the erection is invalid. There is no invalidating clause in canon 1415. Besides, a suitable endowment will not always imply a sufficiency for the maintenance of the rector, as in the case of compatible benefices. We have discussed the third condition above.

But have our pastors the second condition, namely, have they the right to the revenue coming from the parish benefice? Have they the right to certain and voluntary offerings of the faithful? The certain and voluntary offerings of the faithful in this country come in the form of pew rents, block collections, yearly dues, Christmas and Easter collections, and the like. We have said that pastors here receive, not these certain and voluntary offerings, but stated salaries, and that the salaries are considered as the amount of beneficial revenue necessary for their decent support, either with or without living expenses, according as to how the salary

---

124. Canon 1410.

is regulated. Can we say then that pastors here receive the revenue of the parish or benefice? It seems to the writer that we can, and that the circumstances of the country permit the bishops to determine just how much revenue the pastor needs, in harmony with the long standing custom of determining the salary. Even if one must concede that the disposition of superfluous goods must be permitted beneficiaries without any interference from their bishop, is it not rather the present system must be changed, than that we conclude that the parishes are not benefices? If we decide that the parishes are canonical and refuse to admit that they are likewise benefices, we shall find the laws governing this sort of entity. Canon 1415 appears to make an exception for parishes that have not sufficient revenue, but where will we find any regulations for parishes which are canonical, have the sufficient revenue, and still are not benefices? The Code, which is supposed to be the collection of all the universal laws governing the organization of the Church, does not legislate for such a parish. Can we presume that there is a lacuna in the Code? When we look for the division, union, erection and the like, of parishes, we find it under the title of benefices.

We have noticed a change in the very definition of benefices—the omission of the *perpetual* right to receive revenue; and a change in the constitution of the endowment of a benefice, so as to include, for example, stole fees. We have also noticed a new distinction with regard to pastors, namely, their division into removable and irremovable species. It would be interesting to know why these changes were made if not for the very purpose of including such places as the United States under the common law with regard to both parishes and benefices, and making it easier to accomplish this end by accommodating the law to the circumstances of the places. The whole history of the Church in this country has been one of gradual approach to the common law of the

Church, and now it appears that the universal law is coming down to our level, so to speak, to meet the conditions. What grounds, therefore, has anybody to try to evade the issue when it is put so clearly to us? It seems that the burden of the proof is on one who objects to the conclusion that we do possess benefices.

According to some there is a solid doubt about our national parishes being benefices, because (as they claim) "they are actually, and almost necessarily more or less subsidiary and fluctuating."[125] To say that they are subsidiary is not absolutely true, because their standing has been recognized by the Code as independent from the parish within the limits of which they are erected.[126] It is true that the Code prohibits the erection of new parishes of this kind, but it explicitly permits the existing national parishes to keep their identity, and therefore, their independence from the territorial parish. And are they necessarily fluctuating? Have not such parishes been established for years and with no prospect of dropping out of existence? It is not necessary that a parish be guaranteed to last forever before it may be erected. Otherwise what is the purpose of the law on suppression of benefices? The only requisite in this regard is that it be permanently established regardless of whether or not it afterwards becomes unnecessary. Many of the present territorial parishes will most likely lose most or all of their present parishioners when economic conditions in this district change. We think, then, that even the national parishes have equally as much right to the name canonical parish and benefice as the territorial parish, provided the other conditions are present. According to the decree of the Sacred Congregation of the Consistory,[127] above cited, there is mentioned as subsidiary churches, those churches which, on

---

125. Augustine, *op. cit.*, Vol. VI, page 495.
126. Canon 216, 4.
127. 1 August, 1919.

account of the small number of people or of the fluctuating population, or absolute lack of suitable means of support cannot be erected into parishes. The fluctuating population here mentioned cannot be applied to national parishes, because members of national parishes are no more of a fluctuating nature in this country than the members of the territorial parish. The only difference is one of language and their residence is as permanently fixed as that of those who at present speak the vernacular tongue.

We are forced, therefore, to the conclusion that, at least in the vast majority of the parishes of the country, are found all the necessary elements for benefices, and it is well nigh impossible to adduce arguments which will weaken this conclusion.

BIBLIOGRAPHY

Sources

Acta Apostolicae Sedis, Romae, 1909-1921.

Acta ed Decreta Concilii Plenarii Baltimorensis II, Baltimore, 1868.

Acta et Decreta Concilii Plenarii Baltimorensis III, Baltimore, 1886.

Acta Sanctae Sedis, Romae, 1865-1906.

American Ecclesiastical Review, Philadelphia,

Catholic Encyclopedia, New York, 1911.

Canones et Decreta Concilii Tridentini, Romae, 1914.

Canoniste Contemporain.

Codex Juris Canonici, Romae, 1917.

Collectanea S. Congregationis de Propaganda Fide, Romae, 1907.

Constitutiones Dioceseos Bostonensis, Sixth Synod, Boston, 1919.

Corpus Juris Canonici, Lipsiae, 1839.

Irish Ecclesiastical Record, Dublin.

Homeletic Monthly and Pastoral Review, New York.

Irish Theological Quarterly.

Authors

Alphonsus, "*Theologiae Moralis*," Ratisbonae, 1846.

Andre, "*Dictionnaire de Droit Canonique*," Paris, 1844.

Argento, "*Dissertationes Tres de Re Beneficiaria*," Naples, 1708.

Augustine, "*A Commentary on Canon Law*," St. Louis, 1919-1921.

Ayrinhac, "*Penal Legislation in the New Code of Canon Law*," New York, 1920.

Baart, "*Legal Formulary*," New York, 1898.

Bargilliat, "*Praelectiones Juris Canonici,*" Parisiis, 1915.

Bargilliat, "*Droits et Devoirs des Cures et des Vicaires paroissiaux,* Paris, 1919.

Berardi, "*Compendium de Parocho,*" Faventiae, 1887.

Blat, "*Commentarium Textus Codicis Juris Canonici,*" Romae, 1919.

Bouix, "*Tractatus de Parocho,*" Parisiis, 1880.
"*Tractatus de Curia Romana,*" Parisiis, 1880.

Capello, "*De Curia Romana,*" Romae, 1913.

Creusen-Vermeersch, "*Summa Novi Juris Canonici,*" Mechliniae, 1919.

D'Annibale, "*Summa Theologiae Moralis,*" Romae, 1891.

De Angelis, "*Praelectiones Juris Canonici,*" Romae, 1877.

De Luca, "*Summa Praelectionum in Libros Decretalium,*" Prati, 1904.

Devoti, "*Libri IV Institutionum Canonicarum,*" Leodii, 1860.

Encyclopedia Britannica, Articles "Benefice," etc., Eleventh Edition.

Encyclopedie, La Grande, Articles "Benefice" "Beneficiaire," etc., Paris.

Fagnanus, "*Jus Canonicum,*" Coloniae, 1676-1682.

Feije, "*De Beneficiis,*" Romae.

Ferraris, "*Prompta Bibliotheca,*" Parisiis, 1865.

Ferreres, "*Institutiones Canonicae,*" Barcinone, 1917.
"*Compendium Theologiae Moralis,*" Barcinone, 1919.

Garcia, "*De Beneficiis Ecclesiasticis,*" Venetiis, 1618.

Genicot, "*Theologiae Moralis Institutiones,*" Lovanii, 1905.

Gennari-Bouhinhon, "*Consultationes de Morale, de Droit Canonique, et de Liturgie,* Paris, 1907.

Goschler, *Encyclopedie de la Theologie Catholique, Articles "Benefice Ecclesiastique," etc.,*

Gury, "*Compendium Theologiae Moralis,*" Parisiis, 1862.

Hilling, "*Procedure at the Roman Curia,*" New York, 1907.

Konings, "*Commentarium in Facultates Apostolicas,*" New York, 1886.

Lehmkuhl, "*Theologiae Moralis,*" Friburgi Brisgoviae, 1910.

Leurenius, "*Forum Beneficiale,*" Venetiis, 1742.

Murray, "*The Present Juridical Status of Parishes in the United States,*" Catholic University of America, 1919.

Meehan, "*Compendium Juris Canonici,*" Roffae, 1899.

Noldin, "*Summa Theologiae Moralis,*" Oeniponte, 1914.

Pastore, "*Tractatus de Beneficiis et Censuris Ecclesiasticis,*" Tolosae, 1675.

Pirhing, "*Jus Canonicum in V Libros Decretalium,*" Dillingae, 1674.

Putzer, "*Commentarium in Facultates Apostolicas,*" New York, 1898.

Reiffenstuehl, "*Jus Canonicum Universum,*" Parisiis, 1864-1867.

Sagmuller, "*Lehrbuch des Katholischen Kirchenrechts,*" Friburgi, Brisgoviae, 1909.

Schmalzgrueber, "*Jus Canonicum Universum,*" Romae, 1843-1845.

Santi-Leitner, "*Praelectiones Juris Canonici,*" Ratisbonae, 1898.

Soglia, "*Institutiones Juris Privati Ecclesiastici,*" Parisiis.

Sebastianelli, "*Praelectiones Juris Canonici,*" Romae, 1905.

Shea, "*History of the Catholic Church in the United States,*" New York, 1892.

Smith, "*Elements of Ecclesiastical Law,*" New York, 1887.

Smith, "*Compendium Juris Canonici,*" New York, 1890.

Schaff-Herzog, "*Encyclopedia of Religious Knowledge,*" New York, 1887.
Vecchiotti, "*Institutiones Canonicae,*" Augustae Taruinorum, 1886.
Wernz, "*Jus Decretalium, Tomus II,*" Prati, 1915.
"*Tomus III,*" Romae, 1901.
"*Tomus V,*" Prati, 1914.
Woywood, "*The New Canon Law,*" New York, 1918.
Zitelli, "*Apparatus Juris Ecclesiastici,*" Romae, 1888.

Universitas Catholica Americae

Washington, D. C.

Sacra Facultas Theologica

1920-1921

No. 10

DEUS LUX MEA

CANONES

QUOS

AD DOCTORATUS GRADUM

IN

JURE CANONICO

Apud Universitatem Catholicam Americae

CONSEQUENDUM

PUBLICE PROPUGNABIT

HENRICUS FRANCISCUS GOLDEN

SACERDOS ARCHIDIOECESIS

PHILADELPHIENSIS JURIS CANONICI

LICENTIATUS

1. Canones 1-7. Normae Generales.
2. Canones 8-24. De Legibus Ecclesiasticis.
3. Canones 25-30. De Consuetudiue.
4. Canones 80-86. De Dispensationibus.
5. Canones 87-89. De Personis.
6. Canones 90-95. De Domiciliis et quasi-Domiciliis.
7. Canones 111-117. De Incardinatione.
8. Canones 145. De Notione Officii Ecclesiastici.
9. Canones 147-151. De Provisione Officiorum Ecclesiasticorum.
10. Canones 52-159. De Libera Collatione Officiorum.
11. Canones 183-195. De Amissione Officiorum Ecclesiasticorum.
12. Canones 216. De Divisione Diocesis.
13. Canones 385-390. De Examinatoribus Synodolibus et Parochis Consultoribus.
14. Canones 451-461. De Parochis.
15. Canones 471-478. De Vicariis Paroecialibus.
16. Canones 738-744. De Ministro Baptismi.
17. Canones 782-785. De Ministro Confirmationis.
18. Canones 801-813. De Sacerdote Missae Sacrificium Celebrante.
19. Canones 871-892. De Ministro Sacramenti Poenitentiae.
20. Canones 893-900. De Reservatione Peccatorum.
21. Canones 901-907. De Subjecto Sacramenti Poenitentiae.
22. Canones 940-944. De Subjecto Extremae Unctionis.
23. Canones 1012-1018. De Notione Matrimonii Sacramenti.
24. Canones 1035-1042. De Impedimentis in Genere.
25. Canones 1042-1045. De Potestate Ordinarii et Sacerdotum in Dispensationibus Matrimonialibus.
26. Canones 1067. De Impedimento Aetatis.
27. Canones 1070-1071. De Impedimento Disparitatis Cultus.

28. Canones 1076 et 96. De Impedimento Consanguinitatis.
29. Canones 1079 et 97. De Impedimento Affinitatis.
30. Canones 1078. De Impedimento Publicae Honestatis.
31. Canones 1059 et 1080. De Impedimento Cognationis Legalis.
32. Canones 1094-1103. De Forma Celebrationis Matrimonii.
33. Canones 1118-1127. De Dissolutione Vinculi Matrimonii.
34. Canones 1128-1132. De Separatione Tori, Mensae et Habitationis.
35. Canones 1250-1254. De Abstinentia et Jejunio.
36. Canones 1327-1328. De Divini Verbi Praedicatione.
37. Canones 1409-1413. De Notione Beneficii.
38. Canones 1414-1418. De Constitutione Seu Erectione Beneficiorum.
39. Canones 1419-1430. De Unione, Translatione Divisione, Dismembratione Conversione et Suppressione Beneficiorum.
40. Canones 1431-1447. De Collatione Beneficiorum.
41. Canones 1472-1483. De Juribus et Obligationibus Beneficiariorum.
42. Canones 1484-1488. De Dimissione et Permutatione Beneficiorum.
43. Canones 1552. De Notione Judicii Ecclesiastici.
44. Canones 1556-1558. De Foro Competenti.
45. Canones 1560. De Foro Necessario.
46. Canones 1561-1568. De Foro Libero.
47. Canones 1594-1596. De Tribunali Ordinario Secundae Instantiae.
48. Canones 1636-1639. De Loco et Tempore Judicii.
49. Canones 1690-1692. De Mutuis Petitionibus.
50. Canones 1990-1992. De Casibus Matrimonialibus Exceptis a Regulis Ordinariis.

51. Canones 2147-2156. De Modo Procedeudi in Remotione Parochorum Inamovibilium.
52. Canones 2157-2161. De Modo Procedendi in Remotione Parochorum Amovibilium.
53. Canones 2162-2167. De Modo Procedendi in Translatione Parochorum.
54. Canones 2168-2175. De Modo Procedendi Contra Clericos non Residentes.
55. Canones 2195-2198. De Natura Delicti ejusque Divisione.
56. Canones 2215-2219. De Poenarum Notione, Speciebus, Interpretatione atque Applicatione.
57. Canones 2241-2242. De Notione Consurarum.
58. Canones 2286-2290. De Poenis Vindicativis.
59. Canones 2306-2311. De Remediis Poenalibus.
60. Canones 2390-2403. De Delictis in Collatione, Susceptione, et Dimissione dignitatum, Officiorum et Beneficiorum Ecclesiasticorum.

LIFE

Henry Francis Golden was born in Shenandoah, Penna., February 16th, 1896. He received his elementary education in the public schools, and his secondary training in the Shenandoah High School. In September, 1911, he entered St. Charles Seminary, Overbrook, Penna., where he studied the classics, philosophy and theology. In September, 1919, he entered the Catholic University at Washington, where he was ordained to the priesthood on March 20, 1920. During his two years of study at the Catholic University he attended the lectures of the Rt. Rev. Msgr. Filippo Bernardini, S. T. D., J. U. D., in canon law; of the Very Rev. John A. Ryan, S. T. D., in moral theology; and of the Very Rev. Daniel J. Kennedy, O. P., S. T. M., in dogmatic theology. In June, 1920, he received the S. T. B., J. C. B. and J. C. L.

He takes this occasion to express to the above named professors his sincere gratitude and appreciation for their interest in his work and for their many acts of kindness to him. In particular, he wishes to acknowledge his indebtedness to Monsignor Bernardini, to whom he credits whatever merit may be found in this work.

www.ingramcontent.com/pod-product-compliance
Lightning Source LLC
LaVergne TN
LVHW050203080826
844660LV00012B/341

* 9 7 8 0 8 1 3 2 2 2 0 1 1 *